Sue

Sue Rine :)

SERENITY

DON'T LEAVE HOME WITHOUT IT

Learn a simple, instant formula which will give you everything you really wanted in life and become the person you were meant to be. Read how you have been wasting a God-given life force within you and now start living.

All the wisdom of the ancient sages easily explained into a new simple method of behaviour.

SERENITY

DON'T LEAVE HOME WITHOUT IT

Philip Sayetta Jacobs

AIDAN ELLIS

First published in the United Kingdom by
Aidan Ellis Publishing
Cobb House, Nuffield, Henley on Thames, Oxon. RG9 5RT

First edition 1992

A CIP catalogue record for this book is available from the
British Library

Photoset by GCS, Waterdene House, Water Lane,
Leighton Buzzard, Beds. LU7 7AW
in 12pt Times Roman
Printed in Great Britain by
Martin's of Berwick, Berwick upon Tweed TD15 1RS

*This book is dedicated to
my wife, Lucille, whose
spontaneous happiness
and genuine affection for
others is its inspiration*

CONTENTS

Only after knowing the goal of perfection where one should dwell, can one have a definite purpose in life.

Only after having a definite purpose in life can one achieve calmness of mind.

Only after having achieved calmness of mind, can one have peaceful repose.

Only after having peaceful repose can one begin to think.

Only after one has learned to think, can one achieve knowledge.

There are a foundation and a superstructure in the constitution of things, and a beginning and an end in the course of events.

Therefore to know the proper sequence or relative order of things is the beginning of wisdom.

CONFUCIOUS

Introduction

No deep philosophy is intended in this book, although my simple formula for the cure of practically all of life's stresses was inspired by following the teachings of the ancient philosophers. Each of them has some lesson for us. I have confirmed by my own judgement and practice that the technique I have derived from their reflective genius can produce a tranquillity of thought and temperament out of all proportion to any expectation. It bestows on the reader the distinctive mark of contentment, serenity.

I have observed, in accordance with my own experience, that my advice has a proven impact on others, who have been inspired by the apparent simplicity of the logic of my formula to attain serenity for the remainder of their lives. Nothing is more desirable than to secure a perfected method of living.

As a result of this practice they have been able to transform their lives from everyday mediocrity to the discovery of the essential ingredients of happiness.

It is my purpose to persuade you, perhaps victims of day-to-day frustrations and unhappy for reasons you cannot significantly determine, that the recipe for happiness is within your reach. It can easily be learned and simply practised.

This book can be used as a practical guide to living serenely by adopting a new direction. Everyone prefers happiness (I do not believe any of us would choose unhappiness) but most of us have a mistaken method of achieving it.

I believe this book will help you create the circumstances necessary for the attainment of true serenity.

Philip Sayetta Jacobs
January, 1992

The Path to Serenity

I

Many people are continually searching for a permanent solution to their problems, imaginary or otherwise. They find they cannot manage the pressures and stresses created by the circumstances of their daily life. Many are facing emotional distress; some find it increasingly difficult to cope with life; others descend into a depression which prevents them from enjoying general happiness. Their lives and emotions are uncontrollable, tranquillity and serenity escape them. They focus only on themselves and their immediate problems.

They are dissatisfied that, regardless of having the full use of their faculties, they are missing the best of life, which others seem to have secured effortlessly. The resulting disappointments incline them towards an envy of those who possess an immense source of happiness, but whom they believe are in no way superior to them.

Unhappiness is experienced by many people who have failed to find an explanation for the lack of fulfilment in the new world of hustle and rush, and simply do not have time to solve their day-to-day problems. This adds to their discontentment, fills them with a sense of injustice and, maybe, inferiority to those they habitually associate with.

They would prefer to improve their lives for the better, but are at a loss to know how. They know there is another life within their reach, but do not know how to find it. They are well aware that there are people who seem to enjoy an inner contentment, who are always in full control of their emotions, and who never show signs of anxiety or depression. Not only do they appear to radiate a relaxed calmness and confidence, but they seem to achieve it without effort. These people seem to concentrate less on themselves and more on others. They have the quality of reducing their opinion of their own value, and increasing their appreciation of the people around them.

Without serenity, a person lacks the peace of mind and tranquillity necessary to fight the stress problems they encounter in their lives. They have not learned to cultivate a casual, but precise and efficient, calm approach to their daily routines. Most people are convinced that there is a happier and more successful way of living other than their present way of life. If they could become serenity-conscious, an entire new world of meaning and opportunity would open up to them.

How can you alter your life to correspond to the behaviour of these people you so much admire? What changes do you have to make in your own life to ensure yourself a happy and abundant future? Very little, as this book will explain, and with almost no effort.

No one can predict exactly which path the future will take, but each of us has the opportunity to either change the direction of our journey through life to achieve our dreams or, like most people, adopt a muddle-through complacency without taking any steps to create an inner peace, not realizing that life could be lived simply, very simply.

For some people the recognized measure of achievement, a successful business and the monetary rewards which accompany it, are not sufficient for them. They seek personal achievement through meaningful activities which are more challenging to them than their business career and the frustrations which accompany it. This book is for people who know there is more to life than the acquisition of large fortunes and who do not suffer from the false notion that the possession of more money brings more happiness. They have the experience to understand that in the final analysis real happiness comes from what you are and not from what you have. This book is for the businessman who rejects being wholly absorbed in the vicious circle of money-making and finds himself too restless, nervous and uneasy to enjoy whatever success he has.

Nobody on his death-bed ever said that he wished he had spent more time on his business. On the contrary he is more likely to regret having spent too much time on his business and less on other values.

You may be unaware that there exists a simple method of behaviour, the practice of which will give you the serenity everybody secretly and sub-consciously longs for and which could accompany you through your daily routine. It could unlock a secret door to a new and richer life and give you a feeling of contentment and success which could erase your destructive tensions. Up to the present moment you would never have believed this possible. What could be better than to live out the rest of your life serenely and in complete possession of yourself, to have things go smoothly and pleasantly without the emotional stresses, worry, fear and frustrations which prevent so many from having the happiness they deserve.

Serenity is the only quality in our lives which is so easily obtained and makes life worth living. Without it you could be an easy victim of excessive anxiety and depression. Yet how many of us have it? No one lives their life more fully than the person who is relaxed, calm and able to overcome stressful tendencies, being emotionally prepared in an instant to meet any problem which may suddenly appear. These people are serene in the knowledge that they have a course in life clearly embedded in their minds. They have a confident attitude to living and their self-reliance adorns them with dignity, enabling them to rise above all the adverse conditions, trials and tribulations they encounter in their lives. They know the importance of self-reliance, which allows no adversity to alter their slow, steady pace.

These people have a serenity within them that shines upon everything, and this inner serenity is the reason for their happiness. It is not events and possessions which produce happiness, it is a state of mind which can endow events with a serene quality, and the cultivation and continuation of this state is what we should try to maintain. This state of mind can be so easily acquired by a very simple technique. It is a clear-cut and concise method of achieving serenity, yet how many of your acquaintances are endowed with this gift? The fortunate possessors of it have a rare quality in their lives; they have poise and confidence and are in harmony with themselves.

This book will direct you to a happy and prosperous life and will free you of any mediocrity which may have a disturbing influence on your life. To possess all the riches in the world is not fulfilling if you do not also possess the peace of mind to enjoy them. If you have this gift, success in whatever area you desire will be magnetically attracted to you and without effort your new, relaxed mind will subconsciously supply you with all the ingredients to fulfil your ambitions. Just as locating the missing pieces of a jig-saw puzzle is necessary for its completion, your mind will function likewise. Unfortunately, because of our problems and tensions, many of us unintentionally drive the serenity we deserve completely out of our lives and submit to our fate, continuing life in complete disharmony with ourselves.

There is hardly a single problem which cannot be entirely eliminated, or considerably diminished, if you were to apply this uncomplicated formula to your daily life. Problems which existed before may disappear or become diminished. Its practice will produce a harmony within you which I will describe in the following chapters. Making this change will guarantee you an inner peace and physical well-being. There is a contented way to live and if you know how to achieve that contentment you can alter your life for the better. It will permit happiness and success in unbelievable proportions.

Once you decide to adopt this method and prepare yourself to have this new image, the more you will think of yourself in terms of this desired person and the more your behaviour will conform to that image. It is a well-known fact that we are what we think and what we habitually do. It can be easily developed through practice and can give you everything you want in life, together with (and this is most important) the calmness and serenity needed to enjoy it.

You need not at this point accept anything more but I promise you that in future chapters you will understand more of this simple technique to direct you to a happy and prosperous life. We are all searching for serenity. You can find it as soon as you practise my formula. Once it is developed you will be mentally relaxed and will be able to automatically cope with any situation without anxiety. Nothing will frustrate you because you will have everything under control.

Neurotics can have all the material things but what good are they if they do not bring them the peace they seek. We all deserve to be happy and would rather be in the company of happy people. They are filled with enthusiasm, optimism and assurance. They radiate confidence in their personal lives. Generally their positive attitude is intoxicating and their happiness is contagious to the people who are fortunate to be associated with them. They seem to have found their success, whatever it is, without stress. If it had been given to them with stress, they would have rejected it. My formula will, when practised, cure you of stress, make you less fearful of the future and prepare the way for you to produce positive happiness. It will teach you a simple method of mental mastery that puts difficult mind-training courses in the shade.

We all know tense and frustrated people who are always nervously busy, even when idle. They are overwhelmed by their daily problems, no matter how significant they are. In fact, although most of these problems are imaginary, they are treated as life-threatening. Life's priorities become distorted and years roll by without them learning how to enjoy life. Their whole existence is concerned with petty frustrations and pressures, most of which could not possibly be remembered a week later. By then new problems have arisen to take their place. Their idleness is in reality a form of dissipated energy or even laziness. They have not learned how to conserve and accumulate their strength. There is nothing wrong with intelligent laziness when one learns to store this energy and use it skillfully at the opportune moment. But these people are unable to master any simple situation because they do not possess a relaxed mind.

As one acts or behaves, so does one become. He who has a confused mind will behave confusedly. He who has a serene mind, will behave serenely.

SOME PEOPLE ARE BUSILY DOING THEIR
LEISURE WHILE OTHERS ARE LEISURELY
DOING THEIR BUSINESS.

CONFUCIOUS

This world is full of disappointed millionaires who believed that the possession of wealth would enable them to satisfy all their desires. They succumbed to the success-trap by looking for their identity in material acquisition, which rarely provides sustained satisfaction. The happiness obtained from material things in most cases is temporary. Their wealth failed to produce the happiness they had expected and they will have found it was not worth the expenditure in pressure and sacrifices. They had everything money could buy but it still failed to make them happy. They had concentrated too much on wealth, not realizing it was unfulfilling without peace of mind to accompany it. Success is not just accumulating money, having it does not make you successful. If you have lost your family and health in the process, you are a failure. The saying that the best things in life are free is true. All you have to do is have the will to put serenity into your life and to know how to take advantage of your natural attributes to guide you into a better life.

There are methods which can control your thoughts to enable your actions to fit easily into a scheme of life which suits you. In order to act correctly you must make an effort to think correctly. To desire sufficient for your needs and future security is normal, but money which cannot be used is generally not worth the sacrifices required. Such desires tend to make people restless in their quest for material things and the quarrels which inevitably arise with their accumulation generally worsen the situation. The great number of legal battles over disputes about money testify to this. Many millionaires outwardly appear successful, but inwardly they are failures because they found their money did not bring the happiness they expected. They are sometimes cynical and unpleasant company and have an attitude which is usually negative. They are distrustful, and are at a loss to understand why, with the amassing of their wealth, they have failed to find the peace of mind they had anticipated and are puzzled as to why others, who have much less, can be so much happier.

At the end of life's road, too many people find the price they have paid for their success was too high for the product they received. This book will open the door to a new force quite the opposite of these negative impulses.

I hope to make you realize how you have been wasting a life force which always existed in you but of which you were unaware. If people could view all the goals in life with open minds they may discover that they really did not desire some of the things they sacrificed so much of their lives to obtain.

This book is the collected result of abstracts of wisdom which have been handed down by great philosophers of the past whose beliefs can improve your present-day living. You do not have to cling to particular creeds or dogmas to understand what they were saying. They understood a method of behaviour which can now enable you to get the most out of your life with much less effort than you are at present using.

They left their knowledge to the world but in a form too intellectual for the average person. Generally, people are too busy trying to overcome the worries of everyday living to have time to study ancient philosophy. In the mind of a worrier, worries never end. As each hurdle is overcome a new one arises. We do not realize that most of our problems would not arise if we knew how to compose our life. Everybody is searching for pleasures but life does not consist of pleasures alone. These are temporary and a succession of them rarely satisfies for long. There is a difference between pleasure and happiness. Happiness is permanent; it comes from within. It can always be with us if we know how to obtain it. If we are blessed with it, we are set free from our constant striving. A close examination of your goals in life may lead you to discover that you have been pursuing habitually a course which did not relate to your real happiness.

My formula will help you to understand the truth of what you really want out of life. This could lead to a new sense of freedom, where your mind will now set new goals. You will learn to distinguish the true from the false, your vision of your personal goals will become clearer and you will live your life with more assurance. It is the highway to understanding yourself.

You may no longer be motivated by your old habits and by adopting new ones, which will be decided by the realization of what are your real goals, you will now reach a new appraisal of your future. This book has been written to describe how you can have a contented and fulfilling life, or better still, the life you really wanted. It can cure or reduce most of life's difficulties to a minimum, even eliminating them entirely. You can change the circumstances in which you find yourself. By beginning a new technique for conducting your life, you can learn how to fulfil your untapped potential and flow naturally towards your objectives. We possess a vast amount of knowledge which is not actually present in our conscious mind. Most of our life experiences lie dormant in our subconscious mind.

My formula will make your subconscious mind intuitively cooperate with your conscious mind. It requires no deep study or training and will not take any time away from your present pursuits. On the contrary, the practice will enable you effortlessly to accomplish twice as much each day. Your time will not be wasted as you will soon discover the inner serenity achieved will carry you through your daily work in a much shorter time.

Until now, simple problems have become complicated. From now on you will make complicated problems simple. A new type of mental concentration will set in and your mind will work more efficiently, your personality will become more unified, and your thoughts will cease to be scattered. A proper contemplation will put your life in perspective and help you review it to see where you have mismanaged some of your resources. It will also show you how to direct them into different channels.

By using the technique of *Sigo Therapy*, which will be explained in the following chapter, you will learn how to make the most of today. By doing this you will be less dependant on tomorrow. The only way to prepare for your future is to utilize the best of the present. This book will bring stability, steadiness and serenity into the lives of confused people. By applying a little discipline, life will be less competitive and you will find more time for your inner self.

> THE MORE YOU POSTPONE LIFE, THE
> FASTER IT HURRIES BY THE MAN
> WHO IS EVERYWHERE GETS NOWHERE.
> NO ONE TAKES CARE TO LIVE WISELY,
> EVERYONE WORRIES ABOUT LIVING
> LONG, ALTHOUGH ANYONE CAN RELY
> ON A WISE LIFE, BUT NO ONE CAN RELY
> ON A LONG ONE.
>
> SENECA

My Simple Formula, Sigo Therapy

II

A method of mental mastery that puts difficult mind-training courses in the shade.

Resolve, from this moment on, to do everything more leisurely. Talk, eat, read and behave with exaggerated slowness. I have named this formula, Sigo Therapy, after the Greek word for slow. All the teachings of the ancient Greek philosophers encouraged a slow, relaxed tempo for the development of one's hidden potential. You must learn to do everything unhurriedly, to be slow in your movements. In this way you will immediately and automatically conserve your energies and will awaken resources which have always been dormant in you, but never before put to use.

The mind of the ordinary man is generally diffuse, but through this formula your mind will be gathered and you will be able to concentrate in one direction. You will be placid and self-contained as a result. Your thoughts will be steadied, strengthened and increasingly brought under control, as your mind becomes healthier and stronger.

You may, prior to now, have been squandering your strength on wasted movements. You will notice after the first two or three days of practising Sigo Therapy a definite increase in your vitality and stamina. Your body will now feel fresh after a busy day as you will be working more efficiently without experiencing fatigue. Your mind will produce a new serenity and an increased power of concentration will appear. This formula may sound too easy and you may dismiss it as lightweight. You may also ask, 'Why is it so simple?' The answer is that although it is simple it is much more profound than it appears.

This is a life-enhancing philosophy and you must not mistake it as being too simple a formula to have any serious affect on your life and because of this simplicity, hesitate to practise it. However, by its practice, you will realize that until now you have failed to use a life force which has been lying dormant within you. Would you prefer a complicated solution, which after a few days you would abandon because of its difficulty?

Sigo Therapy does not require extensive study, self-discipline or a course of mind-training. I am offering you nothing better than a new life. By slowing down to a completely different pace, you will begin to form the habit of not worrying. People in a hurry are generally worriers, agitated and tense with their breathing becoming more rapid. When you are composed your breathing is slow and calm, and tranquillity of mind is promoted. As simple as Sigo Therapy appears, it requires for the first two or three days a fair amount of concentration, especially if your personality is susceptable to doing everything in a hurry, but you should eventually acquire it by habit.

AS PLATO SAID, "YOU ARE WHAT YOU HABITUALLY DO."

There is no study involved to just changing your pace. After practising this tempo for a few days, you will realize this is what you always wanted and wanted very badly. At first you will be doing it consciously; after a few days you will be unhappy if you fail for one day and return to your old habits.

You may say it is hard to do everything slowly as everybody does everything quickly. However, if you can cultivate the habit of changing your pace, your whole life will transform itself in the serenity you have always subconsciously wished for. Your mind will become more tranquil and your temperament more placid. You will be aware that you are gradually beginning to adopt a casual, precise, efficient and calm approach to each situation.

With Sigo Therapy you will automatically begin to master your emotions, your outlook on life will change and you will acquire a new zest for living. With your new slow pace of life, you will be more immediate and direct, and your powers of concentration will be greatly improved. You will begin to live more in the present and less in the past and the future. Less hours will be spent in time-wasting routines, and you will cease to procrastinate with unproductive work. You will produce a new economy of effort. Your hours will be used more efficiently and your change of pace will increase your mental capacity. People in a hurry generally use a small fraction of their intellect. Haste is to be excluded in your new tempo, because when you are in a hurry you cannot solve difficult problems quickly.

Someone who has trained themself in the practice of Sigo Therapy will conduct daily business with complete possession of mind; never hurried and dealing with all situations simply and clearly.

It is a proven fact that you can be totally relaxed during times when you are busily active, in contrast to people who become confused merely in anticipation of a busy schedule ahead of them. You will find the faster your body moves, the slower your mind works.

By slowing down you will cultivate a very vital force, and in order to maintain it you must always keep your poise. All productive thinking and deliberations are as a result of this calm poise, which is in reality another word for the stillness which is created as a result of slow movements.

Regardless of your surroundings, no matter how disturbed you are by events, your mind will remain calm when it practises Sigo Therapy. When your mind masters that serenity, your environment, regardless of adverse circumstances, will not upset it. As you cultivate it, it will become a good companion for you.

With this formula you will increase your capacity for compassion, happiness, and power. If you have feelings of self-doubt and insecurity and possibly inferiority, by changing your pace these will begin to disappear. This is a conscious training for a new approach to life. Just by merely reducing your pace, your mental habits will improve and you will now observe, by contrast, how you may have previously been squandering time unproductively by doing everything hurriedly. You were dissipating energies in all directions.

By reducing your speed your mind and body will become more relaxed and you will be less susceptible to stress. This is nothing new. Yogis, Zen Budhists, Confucionists and Transcendental Meditationists have been suggesting this in their teachings for thousands of years, but you do not have to spend time studying their literature to learn this; Sigo Therapy will teach you to achieve the same results in a few days.

One of the reasons for your new found vitality and the calmness which will result from it will be the change in your breathing habits. This will automatically be evident when you practise this new pace. The slower you move, the deeper you will breathe. Your body requires oxygen to purify the blood stream. Nervous people do not breathe properly. Their breathing is generally shallow and jerky and so they use only a small amount of their lung capacity. It is this lack of oxygen which causes headaches and fatigue. Yogis learn to compose themselves by stabilizing the rhythm of their breathing. You do not require breathing exercises to cure this, just practise my formula of going slow and relaxing and your breathing will improve without any conscious effort on your part. If you visualize yourself having a slower pace, gradually you will find yourself conforming to this concept.

You will now realize the relationship between emotions and breathing. Excitable people breathe faster and their respiration increases as they become even more excited. People in a hurry are always stopping for breath. Usually we are not conscious of the way we breathe, but if you put down this book and for the next thirty minutes do everything very, very slowly, exaggerating the slowness, you will then notice that your breathing will gradually become deeper and slower, your mind will assume a calmness and your body will become more relaxed. By being the possessor of a relaxed mind, you will realize that what troubled you just thirty minutes ago, may not now seem that significant.

Add to the above the beneficial influence this will have on your general health. Breathing is the connecting link between the conscious and the subconscious mind. It is for this reason that slow, deep breathers are generally much more in control of their actions. Rapid, shallow breathers, on the other hand, are usually fearful and insecure. With your new pace, you will develop the habit of speaking unhurriedly, using fewer words, and more deliberately. Because of your new self-assurance your words will be well-chosen and more convincing to your listeners. You will be less talkative, less worried and less excitable. Now you will begin to recognize your true self.

When we are in a hurry we are oblivious to the fact that our rate of breathing and speech accelerates. When we are composed our breathing and speech are reduced to a slow, calm and rhythmical pace. If we are agitated, or highly excited, our breathing could become fast and rapid, but if we breathe quietly and evenly, which you will with the practice of Sigo Therapy, tranquillity of mind is promoted and your new breathing habits will calm your mind and relax your body.

With your new relaxed mood you will discover that your actions will have more stability. When your body and mind are relaxed you will recognize the innovation of a new power which could help you accomplish what you previously may have believed impossible. You will be less denunciatory and more subtle in the expression of your thoughts. You will eliminate your old habit of repeating what you say; nervous people generally do, to the embarrassment of their listeners. They waste words because they lack concentration if their opinion is rejected; they will peddle more words in a vain attempt to convince their listeners. If you are unhurried, you will learn to deal with all conversations simply and clearly. A man who is thoughtless in his daily speech will never experience the pleasure of living at one's best. Education is really a conscious training of the mind to convey its thoughts in as few words as possible.

The tempo of your daily routine must be slower. Calmness must be your motto in everything; deciding, travelling, reading. When you do everything in a hurry, what you experience is difficult to retain, especially reading, because you learn it improperly, wasting much energy in the process.

SLOWLY LEARN AND THEN YOU WILL
KNOW.

CONFUCIOUS

The ancient sages knew the secret which cultivated the spark of genius in them. Confucious, consciously, never allowed himself to hasten his pace. He claimed he had a central thread running through his body, which was his way of describing his method of relaxing and a willingness to be open to events. A slower gait in life will improve your awareness, increase your powers of concentration and will produce a self-collectedness at all times. By the continuing practice of Sigo Therapy you will be less talkative and more attentive to the people around you. Your mind will therefore become more active and wide awake. The ancient Yogis of India, who concentrated on mind control, believed that the continual relaxing your stomach, which they called the Hara, will lead to a greater degree of mental stability. One who functions from the Hara is not easily disturbed. When your body slows down you will find after several days a new intuition will mysteriously appear within you. If you follow it, it will eventually lead you to your goals. There is much more about intuition in one of the following chapters.

If I were to point to a door and inform you that simply by opening it, your life will change for the better, would you hesitate? Of course not. How much effort would be required to open that door? If I told you simply that reducing your pace would change your life for the better, would you do it? You certainly should. I am sure that if you were aware that changing your pace would give you the serenity, inner peace and enlightenment you desire, you would not hesitate for one moment. Well, it definitely works and you can accept it as a direct approach to the life you have always wanted, but never believed was so easily obtainable. For the small amount of effort which I am asking you to perform, good things happen and fantastic results will follow. Actions only will make your dreams become a reality.

You will feel that serenity and peace of mind is yours for the taking, and that with your new assurance you can overcome any adversity. If you are someone who has failed in undertakings, financial, personal or family, my formula will change your life. Let this book serve as an incentive to open a door to a simple and more productive life.

If you dismiss this formula as not practical, or unessential, then you can surely assume it is nothing more than an unwillingness to exert yourself for improvement. Maybe no real desire exists, if you resist the simple effort required to put this into practice. You may be the type of person who enjoys blaming others for your problems, instead of viewing them as a product of your own past mistakes.

IF ANY MAN BE UNHAPPY, LET HIM KNOW
IT IS BY REASON OF HIMSELF ALONE.

EPICTETUS

Your past is forever closed to you; no worry, no suffering, no despair can alter it. The future you can change, it is yours to change. How does one accomplish this? Easily. By improving your present the future will take of itself. My formula will help you do just that. It is a method of preventing your future from becoming a replica of your past.

By cultivating this new formula you will find the peace of mind you were always seeking, but which previously escaped you, attracts itself to you of its own acccord. You will begin to feel and show a greater serenity of mind, and your personality will be more and more controlled. The following may sound contradictory but, through this formula, you will discover the slower your pace, the faster your brain will work. Your mind will become more productive. The faster your pace, or the more hurried you are, the slower your brain will function. Your mind will no longer be wasted in idle thoughts and your entire nervous system will become relaxed and inner tensions will be eliminated. By cultivating a slow, sure method of behaviour an inner serenity will emerge.

This is an old Indian practice. By relaxing your body, your mind's capacity for solving its problems will increase. A whole new body equilibrium will emerge. You will have a transformation of personality and character. Your rigidity and self-centredness will change to one of warmth and compassion. If you have a problem, you are more likely to solve it if your mind is quiet and receptive. With the practice of Sigo Therapy solutions to apprehensive situations will become clearer. By its continual practice, you will acquire a problem-solving mind and a creative force which will help you attain greater satisfaction and wisdom.

Everyone has the opportunity to use this creative force to accomplish their goals and this force will appear merely by changing pace. The cultivation of this creativeness was written, not as simply as I relate it, thousands of years ago by eminent philosophers. The principles of obtaining happiness are the same as the ancient philosophers advocated. They had their wisdom distilled into one thought:

GO SLOWLY WITH YOUR AIMS IN MIND.
THE WORLD BELONGS TO THE PATIENT
MAN.

PLATO

You will achieve your goals in a much shorter time
and more solidly with a moderate aim and a steady
growth. By performing your daily routine unhurriedly, whether it is in your business or at your pleasure,
you will eliminate most of the unnecessary actions
which we recognize in the conduct of people who are
busily chasing instant success. With the careful
practice of this new pace your mind, now more
relaxed, will be more discerning and you will acquire
a reflective awareness of the good and evil which
surrounds you.

When the mind is relaxed it adjusts itself to a
receptive state and many intellectual problems will
work themselves out effortlessly. With your old
habits you did not have the time to discern the
motives of the people with whom you had daily
contact. Your new slow tempo will help you to a new
appraisal of them and you may discover, after

careful retrospection, that you had been too accom-
modating to people you had mistaken for friends,
and failed to show sufficient appreciation to your
loyal associates. You will begin to see the people
around you as they really are.

As I have said, the past is past and cannot be
changed; no amount of worry can cure it. You must
not attach yourself to a past that cannot be relived,
but the future can have a new beginning if you decide
to adopt new habits. I am not guaranteeing your
future as our future is uncertain, but the way we
prepare for our future could be certain. If you
cultivate the practice of Sigo Therapy now, I will
guarantee you will subconsciously set your goals to
conform to what you really want and your future will
take care of itself. All you have to do is think
correctly and you will behave correctly. Realistically
all of us are the same, it is our habits which make us
different.

Through this practice your mind will cultivate a
new concentration and control. Most people use
about fifty percent of their mental potential and
occupy their minds with unimportant thoughts. It
never occurs to people that a control of their mind is
most important and that they can change their way
of thinking just by altering their pace. Without mind
control much of what we read or hear is generally
forgotten. We know there are people who can
remember every detail of a situation in a book which

they read many years ago, while others cannot even remember important facts which they have read recently.

By practising Sigo Therapy, which is a method of mind-training, you will find yourself automatically eliminating poor thinking habits and saving energy in the process. When the mind is relaxed and held steady in a receptive state, problems will work themselves out.

No man who is a victim of his own bad habits is free. He may live in a free society and therefore believe he is free, but in reality he is always a slave to these habits regardless of his many resolutions to cure them. By changing the tempo of his daily routine, these unwanted habits may disappear. You do not require resolutions for the cure, just learn the mastery of this new technique and you will, in quite a short time, be rewarded.

Of course you must maintain consistency; this method, if practised piecemeal, will fail. All plans go astray if they are not rigidly adhered to.

YOU ARE WHAT YOU REPEATEDLY DO
EXCELLENCE THEREFORE IS ACQUIRED
BY HABIT.

ARISTOTLE

You can be assured, if you change your pace, you will change your circumstances and these will be a positive improvement over your previous lifestyle. You cannot just *will* to be different from what you naturally are. You must be prepared to *do* something about it. Your life may be a complex problem but if you awaken to the realization that it could be lived simply, all you have to do is to practise Sigo Therapy in your daily life.

You cannot shirk the effort required to use this formula. With its practice, you will find you will be arranging your time more wisely and you will balance your spare time more effectively between periods of productivity and periods of relaxation. Your relaxed mind will help you become more creative and you will waste less time on unproductive routines and, more importantly, you will stop racing the clock.

You may find you will procrastinate more, which sometimes is healthy and helps you arrive at permanent solutions. You must not be in a hurry to solve your problems; your subconscious mind will give you the answers only when it is ready.

If you live a life of hustle and strain, it will leave you no time for reflection. You cannot enjoy life unless you find time for your own thoughts.

If you seek to discover yourself and remodel your whole identity, you will find more meaning in your present circumstances which until now only *you* have created.

To compose our characters is our duty, to bring order and serenity into our lives is to live intelligently. I believe Sigo Therapy is the easiest and most practical road to its fulfillment and that, with its practice, you will think more clearly and live more profoundly.

Hurry, an Obstacle to Serenity

III

How to prevent your future from becoming a replica of your past.

The word hurry implies confusion; a lack of purpose. It represents unreliability; it suggests an impatience at whatever task one is engaged in at the time, and a desperate attempt to get things done more quickly.

Hurry is in complete contrast to a carefully planned and perfectly ordered life. It is an attempt to complete one's chores in the shortest time possible. All one achieves when in a hurry is wasted energy, which is a substitute for a lack of a definite method of behaviour. You cannot endlessly make energy a substitute for your daily living. Only the absence of hurry can help you enjoy to the full the greatest gift of life, serenity.

People in a hurry do not realize that if they reduce their pace to a slow, careful routine and move in a relaxed way, it will enable them to reach their goals in a much shorter time; simply because the person who performs his business slowly has his mind under control at all times, is in complete possession of himself and concentrates only on productive situations.

The craze for speed and action leaves no time for the quiet reflection necessary to overcome the hustle and strain of everyday living. To belong to oneself is the road to serenity. Busy people have no time to review their past, the reward of a man who is serene. Therefore, old age does not always give anyone the right to claim they have *lived* a long time, they may have only *existed* a long time.

Haste is the scourge of the overly ambitious, desperate to achieve their objectives in the quickest time possible. They establish a goal, but deliberately underestimate the time needed to achieve it and also ignore the danger of experiencing a great deal of stress in the process. If they had set their goal with a time-allotted plan, they would slowly and surely arrive there, enjoying their life to the fullest on the way. They do not realize that real success is inevitably more permanently stable and achieved much sooner if built on a carefully arranged foundation. There is a saying, THE HURRIEDER I GO, THE BEHINDER I GET.

There are people who have achieved their ambitions in a hurry, but they are generally the exceptions to the rule. For every successful one, hurry will produce twenty failures. Hurry is a primary cause of the majority of non-achievers. In their impatient rush for quick riches, people have often sacrificed everything, often obtaining success with the loss of health and family, and even their honour. Over-ambition has encouraged some to avariciously obtain possessions by manipulation or trickery. Of course, they believe that the results justify the means and they can regain their honour with their newly-found wealth. To their disappointment, they discover too late that they have sacrificed for money the very things that money cannot buy, and therefore, cannot replace.

Their original motive may have been worthwhile, but there are problems with this kind of striving. When you consistently form the habit of looking ahead, it is difficult to learn how to enjoy the present. One should learn to make the present moment so complete and satisfactory that the past and future will have less importance. The past and future only exist in our mind, only the present exists in fact, and if you ignore it, it can never be recovered.

A desire to achieve one's ambition is, of course, stimulating and enjoyable and a very necessary ingredient for genuine happiness if it is undertaken at a normal steady pace; life would be dreary without a purpose. However, if you attempt to accomplish this in a hurry, you can lose your consideration for the people around you who were the original incentive for your ambition. You may have paid the highest price for these gains; and, in your quest to attain and gratify your dreams, have thrown the more important things to the winds and succumbed to the success trap in looking for an identity in material possessions which do not provide permanent satisfaction.

One should realize that all lasting success is the product of slow growth. By its carefully guarded expansion, the foundation will be more solid and will not be won at the expense of our personal lives. If you believe time is money and that you cannot accumulate much if you spend time with the slow formula of Sigo Therapy, you are under a delusion. You will, in fact, achieve your aims in a much shorter time. Hurry has ruined more men than any other word in the English language. It has robbed them of getting the best out of their present life as their horizons are always in the future. You cannot spend your whole life in the futile effort of ignoring your present life in exchange for a possible happiness at some later date. After a while, in the race for quick success, original identity will be forgotten.

The tomorrows of yesterday are today. Only by improving the present will the future be taken care of. Some people are too busy to analyse carefully what they really want out of life. They may have been

chasing a rainbow only to discover, to their dis-
illusionment, that it failed to bring the fulfilment
they had anticipated. They find, too late, that what a
man is contributes more to his happiness than what
he has. With this realization, the peace which they
were always seeking and which had eluded them in
their hurried quest for riches, will quietly come to
them of its own accord if they just change their pace.
Only then will they be set free from the quest of
increasing their possessions, which in many cases
they could not possibly appreciate even if they lived
twice their normal span of life. One must learn how
to improve the quality of living and be less concerned
with the quantity.

No great amount of experience is required to
discover that in many cases the quick search for
money or success could lead people into a life of
unhappiness. True serenity comes from pursuing
your own inclinations and not those of others.

Of course, there are advantages to be had from
riches and it is not the purpose of this book to deny
that or advise you to reject them. It is the naive belief
of considering money the only ingredient for
happiness which this book criticizes. Money, up to a
certain amount, will inevitably increase happiness,
but when you have reached the stage of having more
than sufficient for your needs or your future security,
I do not believe it will increase it further. One must
realize that the more emphasis is put on possessions,

the greater the expectations of those possessions. The more you are encouraged to increase them, the greater the sorrow at the loss of those very possessions.

No one is more vulnerable to failure than the man whose over-ambition encourages him to take dangerous chances. Some never have an end to their desires, and when they are fully achieved they submit to new desires and yet are still dissatisfied. Yesterday's success does not satisfy them and there is no end to their cravings; they are insatiable.

In many cases anticipation could be better than realization. Even if one is successful this may not always produce the happiness that was anticipated.

NOTHING MAY BE MORE FATAL TO AN
IDEAL AS ITS REALIZATION.

SCHOPENHAUER

Does this mean that one should not aim for success or personal fulfilment? Of course not, as long as the present is enjoyed and you adopt the new pace of Sigo Therapy. When practised daily it will bring about an accompanying mental relaxation and a philosophical attitude to your ambitions which will enable you to consciously control yourself and cure you of that absurd time-waster, hurry. Remember, you are what you habitually do. Think of yourself in the image you desire and you will eventually conform to it.

By its practice you will find you have eliminated hurry from your daily routine and will have the time to examine past decisions which, in the light of present perspectives, will lead to the discovery that your past goals and efforts may not have related to your real interests and, in many cases, to your real talents.

You will automatically cultivate that relaxed calmness, serenity, which in reality is what life is all about. To live your life undisturbed, with a future full of hope, never losing your awareness of the present and not being preoccupied with events which are not yet here. No more will you waste time going after things which you later discover you did not want. A good slogan on which to shape your goals would be the advice of a British statesman:

IF YOU WISH TO PREPARE FOR THE FUTURE, MAKE THE BEST OF THE PRESENT. YOU WILL BE LESS DEPENDENT ON THE MORROW, IF YOU MAKE THE MOST OF TODAY.

DISRAELI

People who spend most of their time in a high gear will find they not only tire easily, but exhaust themselves very quickly as they overdrain their energy. If they were relaxed they would stop to determine which of their activities were important and which were not essential, instead of forging full-steam ahead regardless of the importance of the job at hand.

If you learn how to banish that absurd feeling of hurry, doors to a new and richer life will open. When you live a life of hustle and strain you lose the opportunity of getting to know your true self.

> PITY THE MAN WHO STARTED AT SUCH
> A PACE THAT HE NEVER REACHED HIS
> GOAL. ONE OF THE SADDEST OF LIFE'S
> TRAGEDIES IS THE WRECKAGE OF A
> CAREER BY HURRY AND STRAIN.
>
> PLATO

You may be one of the exceptions and have achieved success in a hurry, but it is doubtful if you have achieved the tranquillity and serenity to enjoy it. Without these qualities, what good is your success and what guarantee will you have that it will be lasting? What assurance have you that a new unfortunate circumstance in your life will not detract from that success? Possibly a situation which you cannot foresee. You may believe that once you have achieved your goals you can then cultivate that inner serenity. This is not so. If serenity is what you want, you do not have to be prepared to pay for it and you do not have to forego any time or pleasures. All you have to give up is hurry, nothing else. Hurry will prevent the development of psychic growth and must be eliminated if you wish to find your true self. The practice of Sigo Therapy will help you avoid hurry and make peace with yourself, and you will find that heaven will then make peace with you.

THE MORE YOU POSTPONE LIFE, THE
FASTER IT HURRIES BY. THE MAN WHO
IS EVERYWHERE GETS NOWHERE.

SENECA

Stress, an Obstacle to Serenity

IV

The dramatic changes in our present-day world are undoubtedly a contributing factor to the increased amount of stress we are experiencing today. Every day there are major innovations which drastically change our environment and the lives of the people around us. Not only is the speed of travel being accelerated, but world events seem to move more and more rapidly. The more advanced our technology has become, the more we find that the tendency for stress-related symptoms is increasing. Never in the history of the world have we witnessed such rapid and profound change, most of it in the last twenty years. Some of it may be for the betterment of our lives, but much is to our detriment. Hope for a restoration of the old moral order has been abandoned. We are advised to accept that this so-called "Different World" is inevitable.

In this new world many people live at such a pace that they are literally killing themselves. Our new civilization imposes stresses unknown to our grand-parents. There has been a vast deterioration of family life, and the new life-style of our youth has caused a very great deal of stress to parents who, in their youth, would never have dreamed of burdening *their* parents with even a fraction of that stress.

Some parts of the media are also a source of much of our stress; they misrepresent the news and direct it towards sensationalism which has a depressing effect. Very few present the news as it really appears. In order to sensationalize and retain our interest they attempt to create panic by deliberately distorting situations which, if truthfully reported, would have pleased us. They present them to us as unsolvable crises which could eventually wear us out. If the media favours one particular political party they may intentionally withhold news which favours the point of view of others. They could be idealogically biased and, if it suits their purpose, will promote a lack of confidence in our leaders. If they cannot avoid publishing favourable news which is contrary to their interests, they may describe it negatively. In television and radio talk shows, some hosts manipulate the truth by distorting simple situations to make them appear complicated, while unashamedly boasting that this is the skill of good news reporting. Nothing is resolved by their conclusions, and you are left more confused than them and certainly much more stressful.

The age-old belief that the purpose of the press is to fight and right any wrong, and be entrusted with a duty to provide a service to the community, has disappeared. In the past, facts were reported simply and accurately, without interpretation. In recent years, we cannot be expected to arrive at a decision based on the news as presented to us, especially if biased opinions, unsubstantiated rumours and allegations are presented to us as facts.

Some interviewers have preconceived notions of the kind of answers they want their audience to hear. The whole thrust of the interview is an attempt to elicit only the information they are seeking and to manipulate a response along the lines they want, as well as producing a feeling of doubt about that response. It is what is known in the news business as a hatchet job.

If you question their actions they will quote their latest ratings as proof that their manipulation of the news is good business. If you protest, they will lecture you on the freedom of the press and democracy, their version, that is. To achieve honest reporting is not their purpose; ratings are their only concern and the well-being of the country is not considered. It is their policy to hold your attention at all costs, while avoiding the stable affairs of daily life. They only want to excite and outrage you. Their sensationalism is sometimes unpatriotic, and their insincerity in reporting events differently from other eye-witnesses could well cause exhaustion of our nervous system and become a contributing factor to our everyday stress.

It is believed that stresses are the root cause of many illnesses, and it has been established that fifty percent of patients attending doctors are victims of emotionally-induced complaints and stress-related disorders. Stress, if carried beyond a certain point, can make life unbearable. We are unlikely to derive any benefits from good health if we do not have the knowledge of how to bring serenity and tranquillity into our lives. Add to that the serious damage that stresses, when prolonged, can cause to your body.

When tension exceeds what your body can tolerate it takes its toll of your health through negative responses. This can be alleviated if you immediately reduce your pace, and keep that pace consistent throughout the day. If you do not maintain that consistency, you will not succeed.

Excessive demands on you to achieve your goals in the shortest time can contribute greatly to stress. Here is a classic model of stress; an executive challenging his competition and slowly killing himself in the process with the high strain and stressful job which he himself has created.

A great proportion of stress from which people suffer is due to over-ambition, unrealistic hopes and expectations that remain unfulfilled. It can produce an anxiety which can interfere with effective living. The man who over-estimates himself contributes to his stress, and the first step towards relieving this type of stress is to establish realistic goals.

Too many people find the price they paid for their success was excessive for the results they received, having overcrowded their lives with new projects and responsibilities. They believed they had progressed, but found they had left behind the peace and serenity they once enjoyed. You may think that this is ridiculous, but success has made failures of many men. Many a man gets to the top of the ladder and then finds out too late that his ladder was placed against the wrong wall. I know of cases where men's achievements have lead to their ruination. Success is very often the art of achieving something we find later we did not really want after all, especially when we begin to add up the cost.

It will have been too dearly earned if more important issues were sacrificed to obtain it.

Unfortunately, we strive too hard for its achievement without realizing the anticipated success may fail to meet with our expectations. If we had cultivated the art of maintaining a steady pace, before embarking on ventures, we could be forewarned that the result and outcome, even if successful, could appear differently than when decided on hurriedly. It is surprising how one's efficiency can be increased by the cultivation of an orderly and unhurried mind.

To wish for success is normal as long as it does not mean the sacrifice of health, virtue and family. Money is only one of many ingredients for happiness and those who believe that they can acquire all their desires through it, are naive. From my experience, the purpose of obtaining money is to have a life of leisure and security, not to continually search for more. As long as we are subject to that desire, we will never have lasting serenity.

Is it possible we strive too hard? Do we perhaps achieve more by quiet reflection than by frantic action? You may believe you are pressed for time, but it is a surprising fact that if you relax, you will accomplish more. People in a hurry always complain that the days pass too quickly. They are under emotional tension and feel they must do everything at once. A man who has trained himself to reduce his movements to a slow pace, will conduct his daily business and contacts with complete possession of himself. He is never hustled when busy and deals with his problems slowly and serenely, no matter how disturbing his environment; he understands the importance of his mind remaining calm at all times. He knows that real wisdom implies making decisions in advance, rather than reviewing his mistakes in retrospect. Then it is too late.

Very little observation is required to understand why it is of the utmost importance to master a technique which will teach us to keep our nervous emotions in control and enable us to practise a behaviour which will bring serenity into our lives and avoid situations which cause stress. Only by removing turbulance and knowing how to bring stillness to our minds, can we earn this serenity. Everyday life itself produces problems and you must attempt to live it simply, without stress.

One who has the good fortune to continually maintain excellent health, despite his stressful tendencies, derives very little of its benefits if he does not have the serenity to accompany it. Serenity is as important as general phsyical health or maybe more so. Many people are healthy, but unhappy; their good health has not produced any advantage. Yet there are people who, despite their poor health and other adverse situations, remain in a happy frame of mind. Tranquillity of mind is just as important as bodily care, if you wish to live a long and active life. All health that is not ultimately mental, is not health at all.

Stress is a relatively new concept in our lives, and the majority of people do not seem to be free from some form of anxiety and worry, and are unable to protect themselves from the problems of our new civilization. Worry and fear are the great wastes that sap your physical energy and are the ultimate cause of tension, which destroys the possibility of a happy life.

Surprisingly, successful businessmen are not exempt from this fear, and in many cases, are unable to achieve success without stress. Success maintained without stress is rare and is the exception to the general rule in our society. However, we know that this is not only possible, but more substantial and permanent. The world is not expected to change its pace to conform to us; if anything, its momentum will increase. What we have to do in direct contradiction, is to change ours. We have to develop a practice of slowing down our activities and disregarding the tempo of the people around us. Let them hurry, that is their problem.

The inherent simplicity of Sigo Therapy may prevent your accepting it and thinking it not worth the practice. But you must remember that this easy formula eliminates excessive demands or complicated studies and will assist you to realize your desires effortlessly. After a while, you will feel a sense of tranquillity replacing your old nervous anxiety, and in a short time the absence of stress will prepare you to take action in any situation that you may encounter. It will calm your mind, relax your body, and help you CULTIVATE AN EVENNESS OF HABIT which will enable you to develop your hidden potentials, dormant until now.

With your new relaxed attitude, your mind will automatically establish a strategy for each day as you awaken. You will evaluate every step in advance, leisurely and without stress. With your newly-found serenity, you will not be too absorbed in your stressful problems. You will learn to differentiate between important and less important objectives and will then discover how much time you have been previously wasting in unproductive efforts.

It is a fact that, at the end of a day, many people are so emotionally stressed that they are ready to drop from exhaustion; while others in a similar state of health, or even less healthy, perform the same work, proceed during the day with less expenditure of effort and remain exhuberant and refreshed. And they have the knowledge that their decisions have been made efficiently.

The effects of Sigo Therapy will give you the opportunity to conserve your energies; be alert to your true capabilities and prepare you for each day, whether for business or pleasure. Your time will no longer be wasted. The inner serenity achieved will carry you through your daily routine without frustration. You will find, as your bodily movements become slower, your mind will produce solutions faster and you will accomplish what you expect in a much shorter time than you would have believed possible, and without any stress. Your thought process will have a tendency to be creative and intuitive, and you will concentrate only on what you are doing. With continual practice, you will enter fully into every action, regardless of its importance, with total attention and awareness. You will not be doing anything absent-mindedly. Ultimately, your achievements, by practising a new tempo, will reflect your efforts. If you visualize yourself having a slower pace, gradually you will find yourself conforming to this concept. Your new pace will motivate you in the direction of your choice.

In the absence of hurry, your mind will automatically define clearly your real objectives and what your aims really are. You will then discover that your past aims have not coincided with your present activities. You may find your previous goals and efforts may not have related to your best interests and could have been a contributory cause of your stress. By proper contemplation you will put your life in perspective, review your career and see if you mismanaged some of your resources.

You will now, because of your new tempo, redirect your resources into different channels, and you will discover that you are employing your time somewhat differently. With Sigo Therapy you will be making rapid progress each day and will be following a new path to your goal, the only true one, which will be closer to your nature. And you will destroy stress before it destroys you.

You must constantly remind yourself what a fine thing it would be if you could live the remaining part of your life quietly and serenely, not handicapped by restless, stressful thoughts.

The serenity acquired from your inner self and

subsequent calm thinking will continue to grow and remain with you. The practice of Sigo Therapy will help you, and with its use you will derive a self-discipline, planned and maintained by an indominatable will to self-mastery.

> THE GREATEST THING IN THE WORLD
> IS TO KNOW HOW TO BELONG TO
> ONESELF.
>
> MONTAIGNE

As long as you continue to conduct your life hastily, without following Sigo Therapy, it will be wasted and unproductive when it could be serenely productive. By its practice, you will detach yourself from situations which previously had been frustrating and liberate yourself from the cause of stress, leading you to a richer and fuller life.

> THE STUDENT WHO WINS OUT MUST
> BE SLOW IN HIS MOVEMENTS, SLOW IN
> HIS SPEECH AND NOT BE WORRIED
> OVER TRIFLES, WHICH MAKE PEOPLE
> USE RAPID MOVEMENTS.
>
> ARISTOTLE

The Achievement of Happiness

V

We have often heard people repeatedly complain they have not had an opportunity to find happiness. If this pessimism was voiced by people we associated with failure, we might expect a considerable amount of misery. However, we have heard these words uttered by those who outwardly appear distinctly successful and whom we know to have an over-abundance of wealth. Many successful business-men have been known to make this statement in a moment of truth. In their quest for fame and riches, to the exclusion of everything else, they were not aware that happiness consists mostly of being, not always of having. They had a mistaken conception of how to achieve happiness. What a man is contributes more to his happiness than what he has. If they are fortunate enough to have both, it is an added advantage, but in giving themselves up to the sole purpose of amassing riches, they may well have lost the awareness of that being. They believed that the achievement of wealth would gratify all their wishes and that they would have the means of fulfilling every desire. Too late they have found, to their disappointment, that money did not bring the desired results. A life devoted to the mere acquisition of wealth never satisfies for long, particularly if it is attained to the detriment of their personal lives.

They cynically would prefer you to believe that happiness does not exist in this world, since they, who have the means to obtain all they want, are unhappy. Can we, therefore, rightly assume that a good life is impossible, if everything money can buy will fail to produce it? Should we relinquish our search for happiness? Such people will conceal their failure to find happiness by attributing that failure to their strenuous struggles for wealth and success. But their struggles were for much more money than they could ever spend. They struggled for success, or even worse, the accepted measure of success. In the philosophy of this new world, intelligence is judged by one's bank account and the more it multiplies, the more the respect is increased. Realistically, our way of living should only come from our own impulses and not from the admiration of others. He who lives entirely for the approval of those around him, will find happiness escapes him.

Actually, the admiration he receives is only for what belongs to him. If he has untold wealth, it is not part of him, it is his environment. He should only be admired for what he is.

YOU PRAISE HIM FOR WHAT EXISTS IN
HIS CHARACTER, NOT WHAT EXISTS IN
HIS POCKET.

SCHOPENHAUER

Somewhere along the line, these people acquired more than sufficient to supply their needs and future security, but rejected the opportunity to enjoy the leisure of their success, and obtain the happiness which eluded them. In this way they continued the strife and frustrations which accompany the pursuit of more riches. Unfortunately, they had not prepared a plan of what to do with leisure when it was obtained. They made no attempt to find other mental interests. And they feared the danger of failure which could place their already achieved security in jeopardy. In many cases, hopes are frustrated and plans do not always proceed as intended, which can lead to the deepest disappointment. I have observed men rise to riches, but their success proved to be temporary and they had to return to their previous circumstances.

Even if a person continues his success, and believes that at any time he can embark on a new manner of living with a spiritual fulfilment that his work has failed to produce, he may find it too late to change his character. He could become excessively concentrated in his search for riches and continue to carry on with the very character which he may have previously condemned.

Happiness is a paradox, it can be possessed by anyone under almost all conditions and is not related to one's environment. Although it is not denied that the absence of money under certain circumstances can cause problems, we have to admit that merely possessing it will not produce happiness unless you have cultivated the serenity to go with it.

You cannot confuse happiness with pleasure, there is an enormous difference. You can buy pleasure with money; not so happiness, which is achieved by an intelligent view of the material things in life, and is the result of an even disposition. Happiness is permanent; if you are of a happy disposition, you will always be happy, pleasures are as temporary as having a good dinner. Pleasures are not always with us throughout the day, only happiness prevails. It continues with us at all times and is the product of a mind which has found serenity. Besides, a continuous succession of sensual pleasures never satisfies for long, as people are eagerly searching for new ones, assuming that, if some are good, more must be better.

Happiness is usually the by-product of an unselfish life and flourishes more where happiness already exists, just as unhappiness appears in an atmosphere of constraint and gloom. Happy people very seldom keep it to themselves only, they share it. The more they do, the more their happiness is increased. Having a modest estimate of their worth, they are less interested in their own merits and would genuinely prefer to motivate others to find theirs. As a result they are more inclined, and actually delighted, to praise people rather than diminish them. Love for others is their solid foundation for personal happiness.

They find admiration easy, and envy a condition they cannot comprehend. The possession of a generous attitude not only radiates happiness to others, but in return contributes a great deal to their own happiness. Admiration promotes harmony and affection and is generally reciprocated. Happy people are full of energy, as nothing is more energizing than to have one's interests not perpetually hampered by self-interest or hostility towards others. Being happy in themselves, their interests are wide and directed to many friendships. Being in their presence is in itself a source of friendliness.

NOTHING IS MORE COMPANIONABLE
THAN THE COMPANY OF HAPPY PEOPLE.

Happiness can be acquired by anyone who is at peace with themselves, and the possessor of it will find it easier to cultivate serenity. It will contribute more to contentment than all the material things desired. With the good fortune of possessing it, you will be more likely to succeed in acquiring that which is desired. To have the combination of happiness and serenity should be one's ultimate goal.

A relaxed attitude to life will subconsciously attract the things you want. You will be more at peace with the world and, because of this contentment, will want less. Therefore, needs will be easier to satisfy. Happiness could be merely a matter of requirements.

Happy people have learned to accept what life brings them, which is one of the great secrets of happiness. They will want sufficient for themselves, their family, and their future security, and will be amused by and not envy those who strive after money they cannot possibly spend. They will accept their limitations and learn to put order and tranquillity into their way of life; and therefore, will have no feeling of guilt for not being over-ambitious. Their contentment teaches them that all they require is a fair degree of worldly goods and possessions, enough to give them freedom from care. With the new relaxed feeling derived from Sigo Therapy they will have less fear of the future. The Greek philosophers all had the identical motto, NOTHING IN EXCESS. This reflected their feelings that we should not function in excess and disproportion, but in measure and harmony. This was their philosophy, they knew the important ingredients for happiness are in one's self and can only be obtained when one is in pursuit of the truth. The more the intellect realizes this, the more it is stimulated.

DESIRES CAN BE MODERATED OR
QUIETED BY KNOWLEDGE.

SPINOZA

Happy people have many friends; unhappy people, very few if any. Happy people radiate a powerful magnet which attracts others. Friendship is more necessary to the happy than the unhappy, because the more you give to others, the more will be returned to you. They are never envious, after all,

IF ONE IS HAPPY, THEN WHAT IS THERE TO ENVY IN OTHERS?

Happiness is multiplied when shared, and its very presence increases genuine friendships.

A man whose only interest is self-interest, and who allows this to dominate his life, denies himself a range of many pleasures as the only object of his devotion is himself. Whereas a happy man, whose objects of affection are a large circle of friends, will have a wide range of pleasures as they, in turn, will return his affection.

The disposition of happy people is contagious; they have a natural warmth and their presence can be intoxicating. To be in their company is a source of delight and contributes to many pleasures. Realistically, the most secure foundation for happiness is a reciprocated love for somebody other than yourself. There is no greater source of fulfilment. The intense love and honest intimacy of a happy marriage, together with its companionship throughout the years, is the greatest thing that life has to offer. Any trouble can be endured if you have the good fortune to have somebody to share and sustain you. From such an intimate attachment, a person acquires strength and happiness through which they contribute strength and happiness to others.

The company of happy people could be painful to people of gloomy disposition and usually they will have a tendency to avoid them, as they are generally only comfortable with those with whom they can share their cynicism. They see the misery in themselves and they assume this is a true philosophy of life. Because of their negativeness and irritability, they resent the happy disposition of others and will even attempt to convince them that their happiness is illusionary and have them join them in their misery. We all know such people, they are cold and off-hand.

They radiate coldness and suspicion in contrast to one who is happy and reciprocates warmth and openess. When in their company, their aloofness is catching and their gloomy presence pervades the atmosphere, as they are perpetually concentrating only on themselves. They will be critical of other people's humour, although they themselves are incapable of contributing to it. I am referring, of course, to people whose circumstances are not unfortunate and are unhappy for reasons which they cannot explain. The danger, of course, is that whilst in their company their disposition becomes catching and your personality begins to match theirs.

LET THE DEAD BURY THE DEAD.

SOCRATES

Happy people are usually givers; unhappy people are generally takers. It may sound contradictory, but obviously it is better to give than to receive. The enthusiasm of happiness, therefore, thrives when you radiate it. If you are selfish and try to absorb it only for yourself, you may lose it. Here is another contradiction; selfishness and happiness are distinctly opposite, therefore selfish people seldom have happiness to share, as happiness has to be shared with the people around you and cannot be absorbed inwardly.

Our friends may influence the way we live and work, and could establish an environment either to our benefit or detriment. If you are creative, the people you associate with can make you either flourish or die; you should insist, therefore, only on friends who are also creative. You should have no friends who are not as good as yourself, as they will prevent you from reinforcing your own creativeness. There are many times when your experience alone is not sufficient to bring about a solution to an important situation, then the benefit of intelligent companions whom you know care about your interests, could be essential to solving your problems. An individual who discusses his problems with friends has advantages over someone who attempts to solve them in isolation. But you should carefully select those in whom you confide.

Happy people have a deep appreciation of what they have, accept what life brings them, do not moan and complain about what they do not have, and are genuinely indifferent to what others possess. They know by experience, if they moderate their desires, they will find happiness in their present circumstances and have learned to count their blessings. Therefore, what they do not have does not make them unhappy. Their intelligent appraisal of life has taught them that these things they were unable to acquire, and which were acquired by others, did not always produce the rewards which were expected.

They have observed that success in many cases had failed to lead to anticipated desires and very often, to the contrary, had created unhappiness.

Experience has taught them that realized desires could lead to a never-ending spiral of new desires. Fulfilment, to the over-amibitious, seldom seems to have the expected satisfaction. It is like chasing a rainbow. There are two kinds of disappointments in life, those attributable to not getting what we want, and those to getting what we want. Unhappy people generally are never completely satisfied and are always subject to new desires with the usual hopes and fears, never finding lasting peace. For every wish that is satisfied, there are some remaining which are denied. Unfortunately, the latter take prominence over the former.

Happy people know by experience that there is nothing stable in human affairs and do not sacrifice their present life for an uncertain future. They know that serenity is achieved by making the most of the here and now. They have not formed the habit of believing that the whole meaning of their life lies only in the possible benefits it will bring at a later date.

CERTAINLY, WHERE YOU MAY BE
GOING CANNOT BE MORE IMPORTANT
THAN WHERE YOU ARE NOW.

No one suggests that you should not strive for success, which is necessary for one's happiness, but this success should be attempted in a relaxed manner, without stress, and you should not give up the continuity of such a purpose if the pleasures of achievement are to be enjoyed. SUCCESS WITHOUT STRESS should be your motto; this cannot be achieved by your foregoing the present.

Unfortunately, many people appraise their life by weighing their possessions on a scale with others. There are dangers when we do this. We generally do not make intelligent comparisons and, as a result, we feel second-rate and develop a false feeling of inferiority. We tend to exaggerate our disadvantages and minimize our advantages. Our inferiority may not originate from facts, but from our own evaluation of other people's possessions. Living up to the Jones's is not the problem, it is living up to our opinion of the Jones's which is; to compound matters, living up to the Jones' opinion of us. We cannot possibly know everything about another person's life, we only see part of it.

IF YOU WISH TO KNOW WHAT IS GOING
ON IN YOUR OWN HOME, VISIT YOUR
NEXT DOOR NEIGHBOUR.

THE TALMUD

Here is another danger; in order to suppress our inferiority, we make futile efforts to gain admiration and make matters worse by adopting a superiority complex. We cannot be happy if we are continually asserting ourselves. We feel the cure is to make ourselves appear to be better than we believe everyone else is, but to others it displays a vain attempt at pretence. This attempt robs us of our happiness and causes more problems, as we are inclined to exaggerate our future achievements by boasting about them in advance, to the discomfort of our friends. Friendship should be based only on what we presently are and not on any future possible achievement.

Besides, modesty encourages the support of others, whereas boastfulness is more likely to cause envy. It is natural at times to feel insecure and, when we do, we believe those around us appear more secure than they really are but perhaps they are equally insecure. It is an illusion we should learn to overcome.

As a result of our insecurities, caused by our misconceived appraisal of other people's possessions, we may create a hostility towards those whom we believe are more privileged. By measuring our own lives against what we imagine exists in the lives of others, their success and security become the yardsticks by which we judge ourselves. Because of their success, imagined or real, we set impossible standards for ourselves. This, of course, contributes greatly to our unhappiness and removes us further away from the happiness we deserve. We cannot treat life as a competition in which we prefer to emerge as the victor. We should only be concerned with promoting our own happiness. Only we have the ability to know what we really want and need to make us happy.

Everybody everywhere seeks happiness it's true,
But finding it and keeping it
seems difficult to do.
Difficult because we think
that happiness is found
Only in the places where wealth and fame abound.
And so we go on searching in "palaces of Pleasure"
Seeking recognition and monetary treasure,
Unaware that happiness is just a "state of mind"
Within the reach of everyone
who takes time to be kind.
For in making others happy,
we will be happy too,
For the happiness you give away
returns to "shine on you".

Anonymous

Sigo Therapy will guide you to your real nature and help you resolve what you really want in life. You will then find the possessions of others will cease to be important. You will learn to count your blessings and, therefore, life will become less competitive. This is one of the keys to happiness.

You must act in accordance with your nature; it is therefore essential that we define clearly what our true nature is. Your mind must be used as a searchlight to find your real self. If you do, you will make progress, and proceed towards your desires. Every man wants to live happily, but many are unable to perceive what actually makes him happy. If he takes the wrong road, it will carry him farther away. Its understanding is very important in our quest for happiness; the more we learn about our true nature, the less it will control us and nothing is more important to our lives than to develop our minds to be in full control of ourselves.

With the knowledge of Sigo Therapy, you will attain an intelligent perspective of your desires. By continually applying Sigo Therapy you will reach a state of equilibrium which will direct you to what your nature impels you to do and then you will have a growing realization of what makes you happy.

Your mind will become more tranquil and your temperament more placid; your concentration will be improved and you will develop an inner peace from which you will emerge happy and content. You will be less concerned with your own egotism, which will produce the serenity you have always admired in happy people. That serenity will give you a feeling of being inwardly alive and will lead to many possibilities if diligently developed. All that is required is to make a start.

As you proceed, your outlook in life will become more positive and your thoughts will be more in the present and less in the past and future. The more you think of yourself in that desired image, the more your behaviour will conform to its creation. With the continual application of Sigo Therapy, the happiness you were always seeking will now come to you of its own accord.

MEN SEEK PLACES WHITHER THEY CAN
RETIRE, ABODE IN LAND OR SEA OR
MOUNTAINS, ALL SUCH DESIRES ARE
NAIVE. IT IS POSSIBLE AT ANY GIVEN
TIME TO WITHDRAW INTO ONESELF.
FOR NOWHERE DOES A MAN FIND
MORE PEACE AND HAPPINESS THAN IN
HIS OWN SOUL.

MARCUS AURELIUS.

FRIENDSHIP RENDERS PROSPERITY
MORE BRILLIANT, WHILE IT LIGHTENS
ADVERSITY BY SHARING IT AND
MAKING ITS BURDEN COMMON.

CICERO

Success Through Intuitive Powers

VI

The simple practice of Sigo Therapy will channel your creative thoughts and lead you to your goals.

We have all heard about the advantages of intuitive thinking, some would refer to it as ESP or the subconscious mind, others would describe it as transcendental meditation. Whatever it is, are you aware that if you learn how to improve your concentration, it can be acquired very easily? We know there is a capacity for acquiring knowledge which transcends normal conscious thinking, and that we can receive solutions to problems in a single flash rather than having to examine the situation through a long logical process. If we understand how the creative process works, we can create inspiration and sudden revelations. Every human being can develop their mind and so have access to these powers.

Our lives involve a constant process of solving both significant and insignificant problems requiring decisions. It is the essence of living. How you solve them is important; by thinking intuitively you will arrive at solutions utterly relaxed, and the answers will be more rewarding.

Intuition is knowing something without fully understanding *how* you know it: brain waves that seem to come to you from nowhere and give you a sudden awareness, an insight, into a situation which previously had been unsolvable. You cannot trace the source, but it is real although it may feel uncanny. Sometimes intuition may take the form of a picture appearing in your mind, from nowhere, which will help you come to decisions.

Religious people attribute it to faith and claim it comes from God. They recognize it as being an inner guidance; as if a voice was speaking to them within themselves. They know, by experience, that if they practise a very slow tempo in their daily routine most thoughts work together. This is in essence the same formula as Sigo Therapy. Have you ever seen a religious man in a hurry? He cannot be, if he wishes to keep his mind receptive to inspiration. Religious people believe that you can only tune into this guidance through faith. Creative thinkers, however, scientists, inventors or agnostics, will disagree with them.

Whatever it is, we know it is a product of a developed mind; people whose minds have been trained to become proficient in concentration can withdraw themselves from unproductive issues and identify themselves solely with the object of their thoughts. By concentrating on the difficult situation, their minds intuitively solve most of the problem without effort. And answers will be channelled into their minds when they least expect them.

I refer to thinkers who have cultivated their minds to think intuitively. Very often during the night they may awaken with a solution to a matter which before sleeping had seemed insurmountable. People whose minds are trained to live on their intuition generally do not strive too hard. They know they can achieve more by quiet reflection than by forced thinking; solutions cannot be forced from the mind. Any attempt to do so will fail by virtue of its contradiction, it must not be hurried. You must slowly nourish your intuition to be alert to revelations.

The technique for making your brain behave productively, is to apply Sigo Therapy. This will teach you to think intuitively and positively; by relaxing your body and your mind and slowing your pace, you will learn to train your mind to tune into its intuition. You can compare it to turning on a radio and tuning to your station, which can also be turned off at will; this will open the doors to a new and richer life. Most people would be surprised if they were told they had artistic and academic possibilities and may not realize the limitless potential of their mind; many unsolved problems are because of a failure to acquire a problem-solving mind. This kind of mind can only be acquired through learning how to use your creativeness. When your body slows down, your intuition will mysteriously appear. Follow that intuition and it will eventually lead you to the achievement of your desires. Sigo Therapy will put you in touch with your intuition.

The more your intuitive powers develop, the more rapidly your creativeness will improve, as you will be dissecting your problems more clearly. The answers will come in swiftly and more effectively, as the period of incubation between your conscious and subconscious mind will be shorter. There are times when ideas are more likely to appear; early mornings and before retiring are generally the most productive times for solutions to materialize.

Scientists, inventors, composers and other creative thinkers find this invaluable in their work. They know there is a vast storehouse of knowledge available to them, having learnt to connect the gap between their conscious and subconscious mind. They know how to tap their memories to provide clues which they apply to any situation, and in so doing, they seem to make genius look easy. They have learned the secret of living; if they adopt a serene passivity and slowly relax their mind and body, an intuitive awareness will follow and supply them with the answers for which they are searching. They have learned not to force their thinking by strain or effort. They know that only by reducing their pace to a slow tempo, will their creative mechanism take over and they have learned how to trust its sudden flashes of enlightenment. By developing your intuition and following your hunches, you could resolve more problems than by logic or intellect.

Creative people know how easy it is to draw upon their storehouse of intuitive knowledge and information; this is probably the source of their inspiration. Others may call it talent or genius. Actually, they have learned to analyze a problem consciously after thinking it out to its full, being able to go no further. They suspend their judgement for a while and their mind then automatically transfers the problem to their subconscious or intuitive mind. In due time, the solution to their perplexing problem, miraculously solved, will return to their conscious mind. These creators may have discovered this by accident or by vast intellectual research, but regardless, they have concentrated on expanding their discovery.

They research and direct their thoughts with a down-to-earth analysis of the problems at hand. There is nothing necessarily intellectual about this behaviour, they merely seek and view every aspect of any situation in an honest and unegotistical manner. When they have consciously researched it to the full, with no apparent solution appearing and their thoughts apparently having reached a dead end, they then dismiss it from their minds. This is a strategy they have deliberately cultivated.

IT IS LIKE TAKING A VACATION IN THE
PROCESS OF SOLVING THAT
PARTICULAR PROBLEM.

They have full confidence that their subconscious mind will continue to search for an answer on its own. This is accomplished after the conscious mind has done all it can on the subject.

It matters not what they try to solve, but once they start, their mind automatically and without effort has the situation analyzed clearly and distinctly. When you succeed in problem-solving the intuitive way, the answers become more accessible.

This is an old Zen Buddhist principle from fifteen hundred years ago. Zen priests taught the faculty of direct awareness or experience, although each of them may have taught the method of achieving it differently. They called it enlightenment, as they believed that there exists in every human mind a creative potential which only a few have developed to the full. The possessors of the great minds in history, particularly Greek and Eastern thinkers, cultivated their intuition as a foundation for their genius. They knew that, with a relaxed mind, everything solves itself in time. Your intellect, too, could be a developed machine for the use of knowledge, but it will only develop if you change your tempo. If you are one of those who by habit speeds up your process of thought, then this is not for you. You will never attain intuitive awareness, as it is beyond conscious thinking. It comes only from your subconscious and that can be nourished by altering your speed; in other words by Sigo Therapy.

By the cultivation of your intuition, your mind will give you the answers to your problems often when you are occupied with other matters and least expect it. Your problems, no matter hwo complicated, may now solve themselves.

Although such revelations are sudden, the preparation for them through the systematic training of Sigo Therapy is gradual and must not be hastened. You must concentrate on the problems at hand, but you must always be relaxed. Preparation alone will not always be sufficient, but it will provide a condition for its achievement. By giving full attention, even to the smallest task, you will develop the power of concentration which will lead to intuition.

A re-ordering process takes place in the brain. It is a creative process which may be compared to incubation. You concentrate on the particular object in which you are interested, you define clearly every aspect of the situation or problem and examine all the pros and cons until you have exhausted all possible angles.

Following this a period of time elapses and your mind turns to something else having terminated any thoughts on the matter. This period can vary, maybe hours or days, but it cannot be hastened. Only when your mind is ready will it come up with the answers. The intuition is in touch with your subconscious at that level and, therefore, has to be developed. What goes on in your subconscious mind, or the mechanics of your brain during this incubation period, can never be explained. But we do know, however, that all this is necessary for the final insight and the discovery to the solution to your problem.

Your mind does not concentrate on one particular item to the exclusion of all others. Your brain is like an enormous computer and is capable of dealing with many situations simultaneously. But remember, if you have a sincere desire for intuitive signals to contact your consciousness, you will not attain success if you are constantly in a hurry.

AN UNEXAMINED LIFE IS NOT WORTH
LIVING.

SOCRATES

The mind of an ordinary man is generally scattered
or restless and if it continues in that state it will never
achieve intuitive perceptions. Through the discipline
of Sigo Therapy, your mind will be able to analyze
each difficulty in a one-pointed way; by this, I mean
concentration on the problem at hand. A new type of
mental concentration will help you think things
through, as we possess vast knowledge which is not
always available in our conscious mind. However,
the new tempo of Sigo Therapy will bring your
subconscious to your conscious.

When we are confronted with a problem, to which
we presently have no solution, we are often advised
to 'sleep on it'.

Strangely, after a night's sleep, the problem can
assume a completely different form having solved
itself very simply. The solution, appearing magically,
may give an intense feeling of a higher order existing
which maintained contact with you while asleep.
Why was the simplicity of the problem not perceived

during the previous night? It is an inexplicable experience.

In reality, your intuition functions at all times; when you're awake or asleep and even when your mind is occupied with other matters. The most favourable conditions to keep you alert to your sub-conscious mental process are periods of relaxation. This is why vacations often produce an increased state of positiveness. Your period of rest induces more cooperation between your conscious and sub-conscious mind. However, creative people do not require the calmness of sleep to cultivate their intuition. They have learned to live intuitively and are absorbed with it at all times. Their ability to use their pool of intuitive knowledge guides them to correct decisions. Their minds, therefore, incubate ideas in circumstances which others would find totally distracting. The creative person knows how to tap the powers of the subconscious mind and, in doing so, becomes aware of forces that are normally inaccessible to the conscious mind.

You will find that each day, the more you practise Sigo Therapy, the more you will gain in power. Through your new tempo and a new positive expectancy, you will move intuitively towards your goals. To accomplish this, you must eliminate haste, as haste blocks out intuition. You will now find you are beginning to depend on your intuition to make decisions, and you will reach creative answers more rapidly. Hindu Yogis in India, who practised yoga of the mind thousands of years ago, believed that such concentration enables you to acquire psychical, occult and supernatural powers. Creative people know these powers can be developed very easily if they remain unhurried and do not rush their minds for instant answers. They have developed the art of allowing their problems to incubate, which is a temporary halt in the process of problem solving. When you conserve your waste energy, your emotions become calm and you will define muddled situations more clearly. When intuition eventually has a more active role in your life, your decisions will be more deliberate and not haphazard and the functioning of your mind will supply you with the information you need. It is available to you if you care to use it.

The power of the mind is greatest when, instead of its forces being scattered, they are brought together and focused on a point. They bring to bear the full weight of the intellect on a subject, which can result in intuitive knowledge or revelation. It is similar to being partners with an unseen force which is willingly and patiently waiting to receive your instructions. Sending down your problems, after careful thought, to your subconscious mind is doing just that. You are handing them over to your invisible partner for solutions. You have fulfilled your share of the partnership, searching for an answer consciously until you could go no further. Now your partner, (your subconscious mind) using its vast files of past experiences, will search for the solution.

As you practise Sigo Therapy regularly, you will master a deep state of concentration and your memory will improve greatly; relying more on your creative mind, which in reality is the storehouse for every event that has happened to you during your entire life. Your memory will now become maximized and your forgetfulness will be kept to a bare minimum. The possession of an excellent memory can keep you in command of yourself and if you maintain a slow tempo, your brain will store the information it receives in your daily experiences. Only by continuing the slow tempo of Sigo Therapy will you improve your brain's ability to return to you from its files what it has retained.

The brain can be compared to a human computer; the most intricate and mysterious machinery not made by man; if you feed it your problems, it will return, at your request, answers based on the information you fed it. If you supply positive information, the results will be positive and will be proportionate to the amount of effort you have put into it. Creative people search for the positive in all problems, probably as a result of having developed a decision-making ability and a confidence in themselves to turn negative problems into positive situations.

Bear in mind that nobody ever loses anything once it enters their mind. It remains there for the rest of their life. Unlike an office file which has limited storage, the storage capacity of your brain is limitless. What may happen is that you may forget to remember, but once your brain is reminded of what has been forgotten, it then immediately brings it to mind. You have heard it said that a particular individual is gifted with a photographic brain, remembering everything read or seen during the whole life. Why were these benefits maintained, while others apparently forget the contents of a book just after having read it? The answer is simple, it was read at an intelligent pace, not hurriedly. The subconscious mind was trained to absorb and retain the material in exactly the same way that it retains all experiences.

Of course, I am referring only to important writing, the knowledge of which enhances our lives and should be retained forever. It will add to your culture and the information filed in your subconscious mind will give you pleasure for the rest of your life.

Worriers are generally people who have lost confidence in their ability to solve their problems and their frustration is a result of their fear that their minds are incapable of finding solutions. The more they experience anxiety, the more remote is the possibility of freeing themselves from their problems. A human being, generally, acts in accordance with what he imagines to be true about himself. If he could acquire confidence in solving his problems, he would cease to worry. He could easily learn to change his self-image by changing his pace and moving slowly and steadily; in so doing, his entire attitude will change. He will have renewed confidence in his ability to produce the answers to his problems, or at least will learn to alleviate his worries to a minimum.

THE NATURE OF MEN IS ALWAYS THE
SAME, IT IS THEIR HABITS THAT
SEPARATE THEM.

CONFUCIUS.

The practice of Sigo Therapy will give your mind a habitual confidence in solving the problems at hand. You will find you can influence external events through your own brain. With your new tempo, a deeper self will reveal itself to you which will increase your capacity to recognize various new energies within you, of which until now you had no experience.

As with a motor car whose engine has not been

used for a while making it difficult to start, your subconscious, which has not been properly functioning during your life, may have the same hesitancy. With patience, it will only be a matter of days before you notice the results. You will now be the possessor of a new power which will have immediate rewards, your entire attitude to problems will change. By knowing how to relax your mind, and with the knowledge of how it performs, you will already be on the way towards using it to the full.

To induce and nourish intuition, you must learn to concentrate on the problem at hand. It is an art of slow acquisition as little by little you will begin to reduce your pace; as you succeed, you will gradually grow. Your mind will automatically regain the power to wrestle successfully with any subject; no mind, however dull, can escape the light which comes from the steady, slow application of cultivating intuition.

Just as in the construction of a building, a solid foundation is the most important part of the structure and the decor is meaningless without it. Sigo Therapy should be your foundation for acquiring that creativity which leads to the serenity and success which you are seeking.

You will enjoy the training, and once the mental habit is established, you are safe for life; you will have discarded that absurd feeling of hurry, which until now has prevented your mind from functioning intuitively and you will have acquired a talent which will earn you high interest.

> THE WORLD BELONGS TO THE PATIENT
> MAN.
>
> PLATO.

How to Acquire Prosperity
Through Serenity

VII

Everything comes if a man will only wait. I have brought myself by long meditation to the conviction that a human being with a settled purpose, with a developed method of behaviour, must accomplish it, and nothing will resist a will that will stay in existence for its fulfilment.

Disraeli

The above statement came from one of Britain's greatest Prime Ministers, elected twice to the leadership of his party by a vast majority, despite many obstacles. Even his oath of office was legally unacceptable in Parliament, because of his religion. He knew that consistent behaviour embodied in work was an indispensible condition to achieving one's desires.

Continuity of purpose is one of the most successful ingredients for success. Many people live their life as a series of detached episodes, without any organized plan. They fail to find the ultimate satisfaction of achieving their desires, which is important if one is in search of a lasting happiness.

The practice of Sigo Therapy offers you an opportunity to discover a new life, which may have previously been confused. It will uncover wisdom already dormant in you, and will motivate you to set definite goals by establishing a plan of action for their fulfilment. It is preferable to set goals for yourself when you have a true assessment of your abilities. Life is motiveless without a purpose.

Success depends on preparation; without it, there will always be a susceptibility to failure. When everything you do is previously determined, you will be more capable of carrying out your plan as there is less chance of unforeseen situations emerging. Some individuals unwisely worship the luck of chance. They feel everybody else is lucky but they are naive. They do not realize that this luck was due to the fact that these people had prepared themselves for the opportunities when they appeared and their minds were receptive to them. Most people allow opportunities to go by unnoticed; however, the practice of Sigo Therapy will guide you to live in constant preparation for opportunities.

If you wish to change your circumstances, you can accomplish this merely by changing your pace. The tempo of your daily routine must be slower, your motto in everything must be calmer, in order to achieve an awareness of your true goals. You will possess a method which will give you the opportunity to have a valid reason for living, which will automatically direct you towards a definite goal. You can accomplish this with much less effort than you are at present exerting, as you will be working more efficiently without experiencing mental fatigue. When you perform your duties leisurely, you conserve waste energy, your breathing becomes controlled and your muscles are more relaxed. Lack of oxygen is responsible for fatigue and is consequently a deterrent to your mental alertness. Also, by improving your breathing, you will be improving your health, benefitting both mind and body. Your personality will be calm and unified by proper breathing, which in itself, is one of the oldest forms of therapy known.

The most practical method for achieving success is to make a picture in your mind of what you believe is necessary to achieve your desires. You must set a goal and prepare a plan to achieve that goal. It does not necessarily have to be financial, you can desire other ingredients which will contribute to your happiness. Ambitions are varied, everyone has a right to their individual choice, we all have different tastes and convictions, but whatever they are, a deliberate purpose will always make its way if you have an inner force to support it. It is not necessary to search for approval of your aims from those around you. On the contrary, such a desire could be a deterrent. Achievements can become difficult if you talk about them in advance, and could provoke resistance from others. The less said, the better, and besides your attitudes are expressed in your behaviour and not in your words.

IF YOU SUCCEED, YOUR SUCCESS WILL
BE SELF-EVIDENT.

You must hold this image of your aims in your mind continually, at all times viewing the picture as your completed goal. At the beginning it could be compared to solving a jigsaw puzzle, with as many missing pieces, which you are attempting to put together. Getting this elaborate jigsaw into place will take time and patience. The objects which are not fulfilled and are an obstacle to the completion of your mind's picture, can be compared to the missing pieces of the puzzle which, when found, you put into their allotted place. The completion of your puzzle is similar to the completion of your aims. When the last piece is fitted you will have succeeded in your goal. Of course, you must have a clear vision of the final picture you want to emerge, and therefore you should harness your aims to that vision.

If you learn to use the storehouse of subconscious knowledge, which I have described in the previous chapter on intuition, and retain a vivid picture of your aims, the finding of these pieces will appear as sudden bursts of intuition. Follow them, and they will lead you to success. All plans, however, will go astray if you do not apply habitual direction and consistency. The discipline of Sigo Therapy will help you experience intuition by calming your emotions and making your intuitive system operate. This in turn will induce your subconscious mind to supply you with the missing pieces.

As you become more proficient, the pieces will appear more frequently. If you attempt to make decisions hurriedly, this will not only produce stress, but you will receive no help from your subconscious. There is nothing complicated about this procedure, the less you force the answer, the greater the success. However, you must retain a mental alertness and a sublime patience at all times as your mind must be open to opportunities.

Of course, you should choose your goals with care. It is preferable to attempt what is within your ability to achieve and to decide if these are the correct goals for you personally. We are all different, and therefore should choose goals within our capabilities in order to be able to maintain that success.

Unrealistic goals are one of the greatest causes of stress, and often contribute to failure or frustration. It is evident that life becomes meaningless without a definite purpose, but you should be aware of your capabilities and understand your motives. However, if you are stimulated by your efforts, you are probably on the right track. It is important that you are sure this is what you want to do, and not what you believe others expect of you. You must trust your own judgement, and ignore so-called experts, some of whom only become such the moment you ask for advice. Parents are an exception, being more experienced and generally having a proven interest in your future, they often know what is best for you.

This does not suggest that one should not aim too high. Nothing is out of reach but it should be planned in stages, and the length of time allowed for each stage should be comfortable enough to avoid stress. You must not forget that your aim for prosperity is useless without the serenity to accompany it. It must not be hurried as success will come through your intuition. If you do not make full use of your intuitive potential, you are ignoring your greatest source for success.

It is not possible for a principle to become a man's

own, unless each day it is maintained, and this cannot be more successfully done than by constantly being aware of it. There is no such thing as a time for it, you must always sustain your interest, and that interest will sustain your power to concentrate. The longer you hold the interest, the more it will strengthen your power of concentration.

Many people do not make one overall plan in their lives, they do everything piecemeal and leave everything to chance. You can compare your mind to a ship searching for a safe harbour; if it has no definite destination it will drift and its direction will be subject to the winds. Some people are always blown by the winds of their circumstances and never arrive at a safe haven.

IT IS NO WONDER THAT CHANCE HAS
TO MUCH POWER OVER US, SINCE WE
LIVE BY CHANCE. THE ARCHER MUST
FIRST KNOW WHAT HE IS AIMING AT.
OUR PLANS GO ASTRAY BECAUSE THEY
HAVE NO DIRECTION AND NO AIM.

SENECA

If you are willing to accept the ability of Sigo Therapy to help you towards prosperity, you must not practise it piecemeal, or you will never succeed. If you attempt to practise it only when you have the whim, it can only lead to failure and will create a tendency to give up easily whenever you are flustered. You must not shirk from the effort of maintaining it steadfastly with constant vigilance. Only then will you reap its benefits. In the early days, you may absent-mindedly return to your previously hurried movements. This is the normal pattern for the formative stages, but when it is finally learned, you will experience a profound self-realization, and your life will acquire a new significance.

You will acquire a resolve that nothing again will contribute to the stresses and complexes you have previously endured, and be directed to a gratifying method of achieving your goal; success will then attract itself to you like a magnet. The result will be a sense of intense relief and a discovery that there is something better within your reach. You will master a new positive appraisal of situations which had previously presented themselves only as problems. With your new discipline, temptations will now be resisted, a new clarity of thought will appear. Complicated issues will now be approached simply and, as you will avoid anxious efforts, refusing to do anything in a hurry, you will be behaving as the law of nature intended you to behave. All that is required of you is to recognize its possibilities, your new tempo will be a magical way to discover what you really wanted out of life and a way to find it.

It will free you of the tensions of business, relieve you of the day-to-day strains, and will teach you to conduct your affairs naturally, as if you were playing a game of cards. You will discover that all the resources of self-fulfilment are within you and you will approach life with a greater intenseness and sensitivity which will produce success in a serene manner.

Success in every aspect of your life is not something you can buy as some material object. It can, however, be acquired by anyone who directs his mind to its possession. Our lives are full of avoidable and unavoidable problems, but by thinking constructively, and adopting an intelligent method of behaviour, you will be helped to realize the cause of these problems, and the majority of them will then be avoided.

REVEALED TRUTH IS FIRST RIDICULED,
LATER RESISTED, BUT EVENTUALLY
BECOMES SELF-EVIDENT.

SCHOPENHAUER

Major Sources of Unhappiness

VIII

Everybody is searching for happiness and it is pursued in many different ways. However, the majority of people seek to acquire happiness by an unnatural method, which is an obstacle and only contributes more to their unhappiness: it is the attempt to live one's live solely for the purpose of impressing others. A great deal of unhappiness is created this way, while we should, in reality, behave naturally, following our spontaneous feelings.

A reasonable amount of ego is normal and healthy in one's existence. Unfortunately, some people concentrate their whole effort on impressing others, whether it be through material achievements or personal success. It graduates unrealistically to a full-time job, which could be costly in time and money. This admiration by others becomes a phobia even if it is accomplished by exaggerating their achievements or, worse still, fabricating them. Their friends are used as material to inflate their ego. They do not realize that true happiness comes from pursuing one's own inclinations and that one deprives oneself of happiness if persistently pursuing goals which were set entirely for everyone else's applause.

Elevating your status will not produce ultimate satisfaction, nor will you reap any benefits from efforts made entirely for other people's enthusiastic admiration. It is not an intelligent situation and is a deterrent to contentment or happiness. If friends, whose tastes and convictions are different, decide for some illogical or unfounded reason to dislike you, you are made unhappy. In essence, it means you are placing all your happiness, your most important possession, in other people's minds and opinions.

CAN ONE THINK OF A MORE UNSAFE
PLACE TO KEEP ONE'S HAPPINESS IF IT
DEPENDS ENTIRELY ON THE OPINION
OF THOSE WHO HAVE BEEN
SELECTED TO BE ITS CUSTODIAN?

The desire to be admired by friends is normal, if it is a natural feeling of affection for what you really are, not what you are trying to appear to be. We should always try to improve our mind, not inflate it.

IT IS NOT IMPORTANT THAT PEOPLE
SHOULD THINK YOU ARE INTELLIGENT,
IT IS IMPORTANT THAT YOU *ARE*
INTELLIGENT.

CONFUCIUS

To direct your time, energy and money mainly for the purpose of impressing those around you, who in turn are adopting the exact same behaviour, is like watching a cat trying to catch its tail. We know it will never succeed.

Unfortunately, some people are devoted to an unattainable object, and those whose only concern is for the admiration of others are unlikely to achieve the desired results. Personal enjoyment of achievements should supercede the pride of displaying them, and an over-display of vanity can destroy the benefits of any successful venture.

Believing that happiness only exists if everything you do is approved of by others is the root cause of an individual's wrong psychology. A major source of unhappiness is continuing to alter our impulses or tastes to conform to our imagined expectations of those around us.

Unhappiness, to a considerable extent, is a result of misguided aims. As Schopenhauer observed, nothing can be more frustrating than to discover that a desire, when achieved, fails to produce the anticipated result. If one attempts to improve talents, or increase possessions, one is more likely to achieve success if the attempts are for personal fulfilment and not to impress others. It is, therefore, necessary in order to avoid unhappiness to discard the imagined personal image, which may be in conflict with true self-knowledge.

The glorification of one's ego, in order to belittle others, will not produce permanent satisfaction. On the contrary, it will create dissatisfaction, as you will have the added fear that you may in turn be judged negatively by others.

The decision to abandon the effort to emphasize advantages and to utilize abilities important only to yourself will remove one of the greatest causes of unhappiness. To be genuinely indifferent to the negative opinions of others, if, of course, they are underserved, will eliminate its .nain cause and can result in a new strength and serenity.

IF PEOPLE SPEAK ILL OF THEE, LIVE IN
SUCH A MANNER WHICH WILL
DISPROVE WHAT THEY SAY.

PLATO

Our activities are not as important to others as we suppose, and may even appear dull. Therefore, unhappiness can be avoided, and in turn can be rewarded with happiness, if one reduces one's ego and increases interest outwards towards other people.

You cannot measure achievements in terms of praise or criticism. If you do, your anxieties will be endless and you will suffer too great a dependence on the opinions of others.

Just imagine how life would be if it was lived daily and naturally without wasting one's potential by devoting energies to attract the attention of others. Observe the disposition of people you know who radiate contentment; they are not trying to sell themselves, their only concern is to make you feel good about yourself. They are oblivious to their own achievements, and seek you out only for the pleasure of being in your company. They have learned that happiness is in themselves, and are not concerned with the task of impressing others even if others show a genuine interest in them, and in their well-being. Boasting to their friends is not a necessary practice to them; as they well know, in the final analysis, they are their own best friend. They do not have to live up to any pretentions; they are not competing for your attentions. Having no complexes, they have no need to remind you of their achievements and will only discuss them if you demonstrate a serious interest in them. They have experienced the quiet pleasure of not having to sell themselves; it is a relaxed feeling from which boasters are never liberated.

ONE REACHES MATURITY NOT WHEN
ONE STANDS DISTINCT FROM OTHERS,
BUT WHEN ONE REALIZES A ONENESS
WITH OTHERS.

There are, of course, circumstances when it is acceptable to talk about your successes; telling a close friend or a member of your family, for example, is normal. Indeed, they expect you to share good news with them. Too much talk of these events, however, could make you appear an ubearable bore and even your close friends may decide to avoid you.

With the practice of Sigo Therapy, you will find your thoughts will begin to turn inward and you will be less concerned about the opinion of others, a concern which could previously have become all-consuming. It will be less important if you are liked or disliked and your wish for success will be only for what it will do for you personally, and not how it will appear to others. With this attitude, failure becomes less painful. If happiness is to come, it seldom comes from the outside. It must come from a rearrangement of your self-perception and the world you live in. Persistent display of your advantages will not bring permanent happiness.

Most of us build up an image of an ego that we would like to exist which, in most cases, is illusory and is created by our desire to be greater than we are. Our real self, which is viewed by those around us, is generally quite different and may be much better than the one we are trying to create. Sigo Therapy will help you do just that; find your real self and relieve you from the competition of promotiong a person which is not really you. You will develop a tendency to submerge your ego instead of stressing it. By losing the burden of egotism, you will be nearer serenity.

By slowing down your tempo, you will learn to use your time more wisely and for your own interests. By not having to search for an audience to perform to you will, therefore, use your time more effectively.

By its continual use, you will create the habit of concentrating on the impulses which are going on inside you instead of on a useless concern for the thoughts of your associates and their opinion of you. This is what is called productive concentration and you will be more self-collected. Self-collectiveness could be described as an effort to retire from the opinions of others to your own honest opinion of yourself, which is the only one of importance. Being down to earth, it will be the basis of your improvement.

Having less inclination to impress people, you will not have a tendency to be over-talkative and you will notice your personality will become more attentively silent. You will find that you will prefer to be a listener. One learns more by listening than talking provided, of course, that the conversation is worthy of your interest. Bear in mind that interested people are generally people who themselves are interesting.

From now on your daily activities will flow with less hinderance as you will be wasting less time on unproductive routines, therefore allowing you more spare time for matters which prior to now you may have neglected. You cannot fully enjoy life unless you allow time for yourself. To display superiority to others will cease to be your goal and will become a way of life which you will cast off into your past. You will find that cooperation works better than competition and you will then discover what has been the primary cause of your unhappiness.

With your new, slow tempo your mind will cultivate serenity, so giving you a new understanding of associates and helping you concentrate less on yourself.

Another cause of unhappiness is envy: people being discontented with what they have, which, in many cases, is more than they had ever anticipated. Being too ambitious, competitive and envious of other people's possessions, they tire of what they have and pine for the things they do not have.

They display more interest in the possessions of others than their own, conveniently ignoring the fact that these others may have problems which they certainly would not want. They fantasize the value of other people's wealth, which is generally grossly exaggerated and will often remark they would like as much money as those they envy; but they would certainly reject the sort of family life which goes with it.

WHAT PEOPLE HAVE, DOES NOT MAKE
THEM HAPPY. WHAT THEY DO NOT
HAVE, MAKES THEM UNHAPPY.

OSCAR WILDE

You cannot be obsessed with the advantages of others and be completely oblivious to their disadvantages.

Actually, you cannot refer to another man's riches without having knowledge of his needs. A man is as rich as his requirements. The less he requires, the richer he is; the more he requires, the poorer he is.

THE POOR MAN IS NOT ONE WHO HAS
LITTLE, BUT ONE WHO HANKERS
AFTER MORE. WHAT DOES IT MATTER
HOW MUCH LIES IN HIS SAFE, IF HE
HANGS LONGINGLY OVER WHAT'S IN
ANOTHER'S?

SENECA

Another cause of unhappiness is over-ambition; many are restless and acquisitive and so absorbed in their quest for wealth that they never achieve their aims. Ambitions are never satisfied because they are ever exceeding. Each fulfilled desire is replaced with a further desire and their hopes are always directed towards the next success. To make it becomes not only a goal, but a way of life and the urge to get ahead financially, with all the accompanying frustrations, is often the primary cause of unhappiness. Very often, the formula for success is the formula for ulcers and heartaches.

The remedy for the over-ambitious is the relaxed formula of Sigo Therapy. It will give you a poise and calm that will produce a state of mind which will reduce your ambition to one of less urgency, and you may find you may not have wanted some of the things you failed to obtain.

By practising and maintaining this simple cure, you will concentrate less on the pursuit of misguided aims and more on understanding your true aims. You will begin to see yourself and events as they really are, which will assist you towards a quiet and well-regulated life.

Keep in mind that nobody has everything they may appear to have, that everyone has problems, no matter how successful they claim their life to be. You must find ways to cope with problems which are a source of your unhappiness. If you waste your life hoping that one day you will achieve everything, you will derive no pleasure out of what you presently have. You cannot continually postpone your happiness for the future. Your present life is all you have: this is no dress rehearsal.

With many people, expectations are such that the past and the future are more real than the present. The present cannot be enjoyed unless they are compensated for the mistakes and injustices of the past with the future guaranteed to bring the success they desire. They have formed a habit of looking ahead and have forgotten how to enjoy the present. Their concentration on the future has caused them to lose their awareness of the present and they are not living in the present world. After all, the future, sooner or later, will become the present; if it never does, planning is useless. When it does arrive, it cannot be enjoyed because the habit of looking ahead simply becomes a treadmill of future desires. For such people the future will never arrive.

The absurd habit of living in the expectation of a better future, rather than in the reality of the present, is the prevailing problem of the over-ambitious. They live entirely to make money. Retirement to them is always in the future as its realization means foregoing opportunities for more wealth. They delay until it is too late. There is no experience but present experience.

It is difficult for them to enjoy the present time, as they are future-motivated and have cultivated the belief that happiness is a reward which one only receives in the future. Only by learning how to get the best out of the present will your future be assured; there is no better assurance.

With your new slow tempo of Sigo Therapy you will live more in the present, and less in the past and future. New values will emerge and you will learn that serenity comes from moderate aims and a steady life, and only when one is at peace with oneself. Once you think correctly, you will act correctly. With the adjustment to your new tempo, haste will be avoided, which will help you nourish your mind to produce thoughts more clearly. You cannot solve difficult problems quickly.

The excellence of man is his power of thought, and the more he develops this faculty the more he will devote to reflection and knowledge and the closer he will be to happiness. The more he develops, the greater the stimulation. With Sigo Therapy, a new mind concentration will emerge and it will work more intelligently with your new pace. By slowing down, your body will gather new energy, which will stimulate concentration. You will then find,

WHAT A MAN HAS IN HIS HEAD
WILL CONTRIBUTE MORE TO HIS
HAPPINESS THAN WHAT HE HAS
IN HIS POCKET.

The happiness derived from thoughts will be greater than that received from surroundings. Life will not be perpetually dependent on what is outside.

This compares to a passenger on a train, intensely involved in reading a book who, when suddenly hearing the guard announce arrival at the destination, is reminded that the scenery on the way has gone unnoticed. Total interest in the book had prevented realization of the train's swift journey. This can be compared to the busy person who is so involved in life's journey that there is no time to learn the art of living.

THEY LIVE AS THOUGH THEY WILL
LIVE FOREVER. THEY DO NOT REALIZE
THAT TIME RUNS OUT NOISELESSLY.
YOUR LIFETIME WILL MAKE NO
SOUND, IT WILL FLOW AWAY. YOU
MUST LEARN THE ART OF LIVING, BUT
YOU MUST LEARN TO LIVE WHILE YOU
ARE LIVING. THE REWARD OF A MAN
WITH A SERENE MIND IS THE ABILITY
TO REVIEW EVERY PART OF HIS
LIFETIME. THE SOUL OF A BUSY MAN
CANNOT LOOK BACK, HIS LIFE HAS
VANISHED INTO THE ABYSS.

SENECA

Of course, we must have a fair degree of security to give us freedom from care; however, my criticism is of people wholly absorbed in the vicious circle of becoming richer than needed, and whose burning ambition has consumed their whole being.

ANY MAN IS RICH IF HIS EARNINGS
ARE GREATER THAN HIS EXPENSES
AND HIS EXPENSES SATISFY ALL HIS
NEEDS.

If you wish to triumph over unhappiness you must free yourself from whatever is producing it. If your unhappiness cannot be explained for any external reason, do not strenuously try to search for the answers. Pause for a while, relax, reduce your tempo and create a feeling of calmness. When you are calm, your mind acquires reflectiveness and the source of your unhappiness will become clear. It is important that you diagnose the cause correctly as its origin may lie in yourself.

You cannot enjoy life to the full if you believe a better life is readily available to others who may have favourable advantages over you; and if you feel that you are being unjustly treated. You will never derive satisfaction from what you have if you prefer to believe injustices are stacked against you. There are always people who will appear to be more successful, but you cannot continually compare yourself to them. Envious people sometimes wish that the object of their envy could be deprived of his advantages so that they would no longer have to fear comparison with him. They would derive as much pleasure from others' losing their advantages as they would from gaining their own. If these imagined inequalities continue to be accepted irrationally, there will be no cure for the resultant unhappiness. With careful analysis of your feelings, you may discover that overall your advantages outweigh those which you believed were possessed by others. You cannot seriously believe you can select your advantages and reject the disadvantages. If that were possible, the objects of your envy would themselves have discarded them.

The absence of comparison with others will produce a sense of security and a release from the tyranny of wrong values, and place you on the road to serenity.

THE WISE MAN IS WISE TO NO PURPOSE
IF HE CAN DO HIMSELF NO GOOD.

CICERO

Fatigue, Anger and
Other Related Problems

IX

Fatigue

Anger and fatigue are inter-related, each contributing to the other. Both are emotional reactions to irritation or extreme stress. When every obstacle becomes infuriating, our judgement becomes ineffective. This can expend your energy and exhaust your vitality and, if uncontrolled, can lead you into conflict with others. Generally, it is the depressing effects of fatigue which cause us to explode in anger at the slightest provocation. Anger is a fast outlet for impatience and exasperation and may be out of proportion to its cause.

Fatigue and anger are due to negative thinking, which spoils our temper and could be prevented by improving our philosophy of life. All that is required is a simple method to improve one's thoughts and to cultivate a new mental discipline, which in turn will produce a positive action and not a disorderly mind.

A man of adequate mental health will react to irritating and hostile situations successfully and not behave uncontrollably. His relaxed attitude teaches him to have full control of himself, which in turn produces a feeling of security enabling him to react positively to all circumstances. His disposition profoundly effects his way of thinking, and he will deal with stressful situations adequately at all times. Fatigue-related problems will be eliminated or diminished if you are in control of your nervous energy.

People who are fatigued can make life unpleasant for those who have to suffer their unpredictable moods and who do not wish to be engaged in perpetual disagreements. They direct their hostility and aggression on others, and assume their irritation and temper are not their responsibility but the problem of those who are compelled by unfortunate circumstances to be associated with them.

Fatigue, if it continues for a period of time, can cause high emotional stress and eventually lead to nervous exhaustion. Attempting everything too quickly, or too many things at one time, can result in fatigue. It is basically the inability to relax, and a fear of catastrophe if everything is not done immediately, which creates unreasonable demands on people. As everything becomes too important, fatigue is increased and impossible to control; a lack of efficiency can, therefore, be expected.

Paradoxically, people who have a tendency to become fatigued will compulsively remain busy; even when idle, they will find outlets for their nervousness as they have a need for constant stimulation. The more fatigued they become, the more they find it impossible to relax. Slowing down becomes a difficult process as they do not understand the necessity to conserve and accumulate energy. It is vital to learn that energy should be properly stored and readily available for expenditure when required. If we do not retain an amount in reserve, fatigue will always remain with us as we will never have sufficient strength to cope with future eventualities.

We may have inherited a tendency for anxiety in certain situations, which is evidenced by our continual search for distractions. Nervousness, which leads eventually to emotional fatigue, is essentially a form of escape from our own inner thoughts: it is a turning away from the reality of our true self.

The practice of Sigo Therapy will be your protection against the conditions which create mental fatigue. Only by a steady change of pace will your life begin to develop harmoniously, enabling you to work efficiently for longer periods. Fatigue will shortly diminish, and later on disappear altogether to be replaced by a new calming force.

People who do everything hurriedly are unaware that they achieve less and that the normal sequence of events is reversed. It is a formula of reversed effort which this book is trying to convey. When you perform your daily business hurriedly, you will not only build up fatigue, but you will have achieved much less at the end of the day compared to a person involved in the exact same activities who has maintained a steady, slow pace. More will have been accomplished with less energy. The practice of Sigo Therapy, an exceedingly productive skill, can be performed by people from all walks of life in order to promote their efficiency. When exhaustion appears, immediately reduce your pace. You must do everything slowly and leisurely and be totally aware of what your are doing. If this pace is maintained, fatigue will disappear in a short time.

Through this practice your mind will cease to be pulled in many directions and will acquire steadfast control. Your entire body will function with greater ability and a feeling of tranquillity will now replace your previous exhaustion, generating a sense of well-being. It is difficult to describe, it has to be experienced. By the persistent practice of Sigo Therapy you will be re-aligning your physical and mental energies and building up a defence system against a relapse. It is a quick practical process for eliminating fatigue.

Anger

An embarrasing result of fatigue is the unpleasantness of over-reacting and displaying anger. While a feeling of rage caused by unjustified circumstances is unavoidable, it is the stressful way of displaying this anger which should be avoided.

Anger can relieve tension and produce a feeling of power; we feel superior to people who have wronged us, but rarely does it prove effective in the long run. Anger may give you a temporary sense of righteousness, but it will generally leave you behaving foolishly. Of course you should stand your ground on what you believe is right, but do so calmly. People get angry when they get hurt; everyone has angry feelings at times. When someone claims never to be angry, this conceals a serious fault; a fear of revealing hidden aspects of his personality.

In many cases, the extreme emotion displayed by anger is far in excess of the cause of the anger. Anger brushes aside our reason and causes us to behave in a manner that we may regret later. A quick, angry response may effect your judgement and, therefore, your relationship with others. In addition it may be harmful to your health and peace of mind. You may have had the right to be angry, but not the freedom to lose control.

ANYBODY CAN GET ANGRY, THAT IS
EASY. BUT TO GET ANGRY WITH THE
RIGHT PERSON TO THE RIGHT DEGREE
AT THE RIGHT MOMENT FOR THE
RIGHT REASON, THAT IS NOT EASY.

ARISTOTLE

If you are unable to contain your anger at the provocative behaviour of others, you must first ask yourself if your intended response is out of proportion. Sigo Therapy will teach you to restrain that impulse for a while and direct you to use your pent-up energy for constructive purposes, not destructively as happens when you give way to a strong anger. In the end you will be much more respected if you retain balance.

IN TAKING REVENGE, A MAN IS EVEN
WITH HIS ENEMY, BUT IN PASSING IT
OVER, HE IS SUPERIOR.

FRANCIS BACON

Your reaction will be delayed if you can, for a while, transfer your thoughts to other things. The incident will then be forgotten until the time-lapse enables you to be in complete possession of yourself. A delayed response will ensure that you are better prepared intelligently to master the situation than if you had responded immediately. Each of us is prepared for hostile situations differently. The same situation which can cause anger to some, may be to others a source of amusement, although, in the final analysis, it depends on how relaxed you are at the time of the incident.

The most effective action is non-action. Quite often a lack of response, accompanied by complete silence, is extremely effective. This conveys that you were right and the other party wrong, and will leave them puzzled as to what your feelings were.

There is no better cure for anger than Sigo Therapy, it will help you develop a capacity to curb immediate reactions to disturbing situations. Its use will prevent you from acting automatically, as you had been doing. The distinctive feature of an intelligent man is manifested in his not arriving at hasty decisions.

THE GROWTH OF WISDOM MAY BE
GAUGED EXACTLY BY THE
DIMINUTION OF ILL-TEMPER.

NIETZSCHE

By carefully performing all your actions slowly, your nervous system will functionally reduce its level of intensity and replace it with a sense of security. You will then cease to be a slave to impulses, and you will cultivate a relaxed and unhurried manner, both at work and play. You will be provided with the ability to cope with disagreements intelligently. When you are involved in a distressing confrontation the heart muscles are given extra work, having to pump more blood to the body, blood pressure is increased and breathing is accelerated.

It is preferable that one lives in sympathetic surroundings and avoids, if possible, the company of people who have a persistent record of causing you anger. Their antagonism to your opinions can be a source of fatigue.

Over-Preoccupation with Oneself
Probably one of the most common causes of fatigue is an over-preoccupation with oneself. People who are increasingly involved with their interests, and who keep them uppermost in their minds, find it impossible to avoid the consequences.

Their inability to accept themselves on a basis of equality with others encourages them to search for issues which will increase their self-esteem; the more they seek, the more out of harmony they are with their surroundings. They have no sense of their place in this world. They believe everybody around them is affected by what they do. They pretend their merits surpass others', and that those of people around them are insignificant. They do not realize that they would gain more respect and save much energy if their behaviour fitted in with that of others.

They cannot be patient with those around them. As they think they are of no practical use, they are completely out of sympathy with them. Their own personal activities dominate their thoughts and their attempts to maintain superiority in all conversations perpetually dissipates their energy. This not only contributes to their fatigue, but merely being in their presence can result in fatigue for their listeners. They view everything in life as a contest and would have you believe they are the winners.

Their discomfort cannot be disguised when conversations are purposely changed to topics not related to them, and they may even regard such a departure as criticisms of themselves.

THE CONCEITED MAN RELATES HIS
OWN DEEDS AND THE EVIL ONES OF
OTHERS AND DELIGHTS IN THE
PRESENCE OF HIS INFERIORS.

SPINOZA

Genuine happiness cannot exist when self-interest is total interest. It can only be achieved when interests are spread evenly, resulting in a more modest manner. If one concludes that the continual display of oneself should be treated as a sickness, this would be the beginning of the cure. There is nothing more fatiguing than being encased within oneself. It is much more pleasant to have a feeling of mutual identification with others and to have attention and energy directed outwards to escape the burden of having to exaggerate oneself.

The relaxation achieved by the change of tempo through Sigo Therapy will be a major step in curing this particular illness. It will result in the replacement of self-centredness by a positive step to freedom from constantly proving oneself. The more you withdraw thoughts from yourself, the more free you will be and the nearer you will be to serenity.

Trying to promote oneself is a result of insecurity; an inability realistically to accept the merits of others and a tendency to regard one's own accomplishments as being all-important. Separateness is an illusion; we must have mutual identification with others. We are all part of a team and, paradoxically, happiness comes only through cooperation and a better self comes only through selflessness.

DO NOT WORRY ABOUT PEOPLE NOT
KNOWING YOUR ABILITY. WORRY THAT
YOU HAVE NOT GOT IT.

CONFUCIUS

Advancing Years

X

*How to age less quickly by having a valid
reason for living*

People of advancing years may be concerned about
the uncertainties of their future, the outcome of
which could be a source of stress. In fact, it could be
the age of anxiety. We have become a youth-
orientated culture and the inevitable process of
ageing already detracts from the happiness of people
who have been brainwashed by this youth propaganda into believing that there is something terrible
about ageing. They also believe that acceptance in
society will not be there as they get older and,
therefore, are ashamed to disclose their age. The
media message which often implies you become a
lesser person as you age adds to this concern. Elderly

people are often led to believe that it is too late to apply effort towards new interests; their lives are over and the stage now belongs to the younger generation.

The real danger is not age, it is negative thinking.

YOU MUST NOT ABANDON LIFE TOO
SOON.

Our culture should encourage and venerate the experience and wisdom of age; getting older should not be a cause of embarrassment or depression, it should be a cause for celebration. Because of the youth propaganda many elderly people are often made to feel useless and have surrendered themselves to advancing years and adopted an attitude of indifference to their future. Highly developed minds suddenly feel they exist without purpose, not realizing, that:

GROWING OLD SHOULD BE TREATED
LIKE A BAD HABIT WHICH A BUSY MAN
HAS NO TIME TO FORM.

Man ages less quickly if he can aspire to a valid reason for living. There is no evidence to support that all you can expect is an unendurable life of boredom ahead of you. If you can develop new interests, which can utilize your experiences to the full, you will be using your leisure intelligently and possibly, even, increasing your income. The many interests and opportunities will help you stay young, and so the less you have to fear from boredom.

Interesting work or hobbies which exercise your skills will stimulate your mind and be a source of great satisfaction. Learning keeps one young. Also, if you are active and involved in your life, it will be of benefit to your health.

THERE IS NOTHING MORE DULL THAN
A PERSON WITHOUT WORK AND
WITHOUT INTERESTS.

People without the ability to find interests drift towards the companionship of people of the same disposition. A man who has a wealth of interests certainly has an advantage over the man who has none.

It is self-evident that, as the years advance, the

continuation of abilities and interests, whether in writing, music, art or reading, can produce much of a person's happiness. With the retention of curiosity, old age can be the most satisfying period of life. No one can expect relationships with the people around, no matter how satisfying, to be sufficient to carry them through each day.

The first the enjoyment of a balanced mind is of your own company. The capacity to be alone is a resource which will enable you to explore your deepest feelings. If you can find some time each day for the cultivation of the mind, beginning with its control, and use its powers to expand your interests, you will never grow old, as learning is the best way to stay young. Some people actually avoid time to think and, in particular, to face themselves. This is a form of self-deception. It is the only way to see things as they are and to learn to accept things as they are.

NOTHING IS MORE COMPANIONABLE
THAN ONE'S OWN COMPANY.

THOREAU

Love and friendship are essential to our lives and their importance increases as we age, but we will derive our main sources of pleasure from continually developing interests. The search for these interests will not only allow us to feel and show a greater serenity of mind, but will make us an object of interest to others. The pleasure of these interests can be acquired by anyone who can develop and exercise some special skill. When the mind becomes more active, it will produce a new vigour and the subsequent enjoyment will give us security and independence. It is very important to have the conscious satisfaction that we are employing our time wisely.

IT IS POSSIBLE TO THOSE WHO EMPLOY
THEIR TIME WELL, KNOWLEDGE AND
EXPERIENCE GROW WITH LIVING.

MONTAIGNE

If one has developed a love for music, it can serve as an even greater comfort in one's later years. Through music, the soul learns harmony and rhythm and acquires an even disposition. With the love of music, one's feelings are aroused and become a controlled instrument, as a violin would to a violinist. Music serves as a reminder of many pleasant episodes and past periods of one's life. Our experiences are cumulative and constantly with us. The meaning we give to life is how to relate to it; the love of music will improve your positive participation and enhance your well-being.

I am not referring to an occasional visit to a concert hall. Video technology can now supply us with renderings of our favourite music played with the same clarity as in a concert hall. I have observed people spellbound, listening to the music of their favourite composer, their total absorption showing through facial contentment. They seem to show moments of superior ecstasy which they would obviously like to experience more often, an indication of how appreciation of music can stir a person's soul and be a contributary source of new interests.

When the heart is moved it finds an expression in sounds and tones. The choice of a particular piece of music could be appropriate to a person's mood. People generally seek music which is in harmony with their disposition. When they are depressed or sorrowful they can derive much contentment from its consoling effects. Music, when shared with others, can increase the bond with those around you. The love of music generally reveals a man's character, he being moulded by nature and made quiet and reflective by his favourite renderings.

MUSIC IS VALUABLE NOT ONLY
BECAUSE IT BRINGS REFINEMENT AND
FEELING OF CHARACTER, BUT ALSO
BECAUSE IT PRESERVES AND RESTORES
HEALTH.

PLATO

You may believe it is absurd for the aged to plan a foundation for a fresh life, but it is the only defence against growing old; besides, no one can establish the duration of his own life, young or old.

Here are some achievers of advanced years who knew the cure for old age was not to grow old. Their work remains as evidence of their vitality and the benefits they acquired from their experiences. They had accepted their retirement, not as an opportunity for idleness but for creative leisure.

Achievers at an advanced age
At a hundred Grandma Moses was painting.
At ninety-four Bertrand Russell was active in international peace movements.
At ninety-three George Bernard Shaw was still writing.

At ninety-one Eamon de Valera served as president of Ireland.

At ninety-one Adolph Zukor was chairman of Paramount Pictures.

At ninety Pablo Picasso was still creating.

At eighty-nine Mary Baker Eddy was directing the Christian Science Church.

At eighty-nine Arthur Rubinstein gave one of his greatest recitals in New York's Carnegie Hall.

At eighty-nine Albert Schweitzer was head of a hospital in Africa.

At eighty-eight Michaelangelo was still painting.

In their eighties W.E. Gladstone and Winston Churchill were prime ministers of Great Britain.

In some instances these people continued to work and create despite adverse circumstances, and escaped old age by living productive lives. Their joy in accomplishment continued satisfactorily, despite their age, and they achieved results which were not necessary to themselves, but of value to others. A continuity of interests is not only desirable, but essential to happiness. It can be found either in creative leisure or work. A man is likely to find more energy in such actions than an idle man who is a victim of boredom and at a loss to know what to do with himself each day.

If it is assumed that with old age death cannot be far away, young people are just as susceptible; in fact, they are more exposed to accidents than the old. There are old men who are vigorous and young men who are weak and sluggish. Of course, youth can anticipate enjoying many additional years, but older people have the advantage of knowing that they have already had a long life and can still look forward to many more years. Age can release us from future responsibilities and the old need not envy younger men who may have a difficult life ahead of them. Whatever our age, young or old:

NOBODY CAN BE SURE OF A LONG
LIFE, BUT CAN BE SURE OF A
WISE ONE.

The future is always obscure; nothing is certain or stable in human affairs. As we get older, we do know that we become mature through experience and learn how to handle situations with more skill and satisfaction.

To send men into retirement seems unreasonable. Employment and occupation should be extended as far as possible in the interests of the country. The work ethic, characteristic of old employees, usually includes company loyalty, coolness in crisis and a more experienced, practical knowledge. In contrast, younger workers are often only motivated by social interests. Retired people who re-enter the work force often make the mistake of accepting jobs that do not reflect their knowledge and experience.

As you get older, life can be experienced and enjoyed more to the full; the maturity of age can produce a great sense of calmness and freedom. By then you will have discovered which things are of more importance than others, and the proper priorities they deserve. You may also have already achieved most of your desires. In addition, many things which you previously believed were indispensible to your happiness and unable to obtain, are now dismissed as unessential. It is happiness as the Greek philosophers understood it; a state of mind which produces an indestructable peace. You neither struggle nor wish any more but simply enrich and develop your own spiritual life. You learn that life is still worth living, even if you are not more successful and superior to your friends.

As we approach serenity, we acquire an ability to review the most significant parts of our lives. A certain amount of resignation is accepted as we reluctantly analyze the causes of our errors and misfortunes and view our present circumstances as a product of these past mistakes, which we ourselves have created. We learn to attribute our negative circumstances to our own lack of preparedness, rather than conveniently protecting ourselves by blaming others. Therefore, our lives are more wisely directed and we are emancipated from everyday worries. We learn to accept things with less emotion, bear our disappointments without being overcome by them and are willing to flow with events wherever they may lead, as our lives become more ordered.

Sigo Therapy, with its formula of a leisurely, slow pace will bring out the wisdom and experience you have accumulated in your past and, by its practice, your decisions will now be made with accuracy and calmness and, therefore, will be more effective. As you have reached the age where you will probably have put your house in order, it will help you live out the rest of your life with serenity, which is a state of harmony without tension and disturbance. If you leave this world without the benefits of its experience, you have never lived. There is no substitute for ability and experience.

GREAT THINGS ARE NOT ACCOMPLISHED
WITH PHYSICAL STRENGTH AND
AGILITY, BUT THROUGH
CONSULTATION, AUTHORITY AND THE
MATURE WISDOM, WHICH OLD AGE,
FAR FROM LACKING, IS ENDOWED
WITH ABUNDANTLY.

CICERO

Fears, Boredom, Persecution Complexes
and their Cure

XI

Fears

A review of our past fears will reveal that most never became a reality and were often imaginary. Our fears may not have been well-founded, but we suffered through them, nevertheless, and they were responsible for a great deal of our unhappiness and the dissipation of vital energies. Preoccupation with what fate had in store for us will be seen to have been exaggerated, irrational and, finally, proved to be groundless. Fearful people cannot distinguish between myth and reality. What we dreaded as imminent often never arrived, yet we endured misery waiting for its cause to take effect. We permitted our fears to torment us, without making an effort to suppress them and, in many cases, they brought us to the edge of despair.

There is no greater obstacle to sound judgement than fear. People who are fearful are inclined to make wrong decisions, as their mind becomes chaotic. Most worries can be avoided by learning a mental discipline instead of allowing ourselves not to be in control of our thoughts.

It could be difficult to control a tendency to exaggerate anticipated problems; what one thinks of as a trifling setback could be interpreted by another as an agonizing problem. Someone could be so accustomed to worries that he is unable to be cured of the habit, even when the cause of the worry has disappeared. As one fear fades into insignificance, with the passing of danger, a new one appears to replace it. As long as we are subject to constant fears we can never have lasting peace.

THOSE WHO ARE INCLINED TO WORRY,
WILL ALWAYS FIND A NEW WORRY TO
TAKE THE THRONE.

SCHOPENHAUER

The more we analyze the source of our fears, the less they will control us, therefore we must examine their origins to discover their cause, and nothing will protect us from their effects other than learning a method to control ourselves. We forget that today is the tomorrow we worried about yesterday.

We are familiar with people who are undismayed by problems, never complain about their adverse circumstances and remain placid and self-contained at all times. They display a feeling of self-restraint and serenity and seem to have escaped the tensions and consequences of everyday living. All our circumstances are perpetually subject to change; even with those who have been bestowed with good fortune, misfortune can suddenly develop. Despite their difficulties, however, they display an impressive calmness and a peace of mind which few of us are capable of.

There is nothing stable in human affairs; we all have to bear our share of instability and should face life with a positive and constructive attitude. If we do, we will create confidence in our ability to solve problems and that will be a major step towards conquering fears.

You can achieve tranquillity by disciplining yourself not to be subservient to future imaginary dangers. Experience should teach us that worrying is futile and only succeeds in preoccupying our minds with conditions which are not yet here and, in all probability, concerns which will never materialize.

YOU CANNOT BE EXPOSED TO THE
MERCY OF EVERY WORRYING
THOUGHT.

The practice of Sigo Therapy will give you the necessary feeling of calmness, making you more fit to cope with troubles when, and if, the need for action ever arrives. When you are composed you are in better condition emotionally and intellectually to deal with difficulties.

If you approach problems knowing that the law of averages gives them little chance of becoming reality, you will become less fearful of the future. This is yet another step towards not permitting imaginary fears to destroy your present life.

UNCERTAIN ILLS TORMENT US MOST.
SENECA

Many things we fear would be less fearful if we learned to thoroughly understand them through a proper, direct approach of their causes and the knowledge that they can be moderated by an honest estimate of their possible effects. Problems are a natural part of life; they can be solved provided you do not get them out of proportion. People who have developed control and self-mastery have a fear-reducing formula which enables them to maintain serenity. They investigate the roots of the problem, accept the evidence and diagnose the origin. Information gathered from dubious sources such as guess work and supposition are eliminated. All facts are sifted carefully to give a proper appraisal of the situation. As a result it could be found that the problem was not as earth-shattering as originally feared. A person who has acquired unruffled awareness, which is one of the main messages of this book, will be able to deal with worries adequately, rather than inadequately, before they appear.

By not submitting to fears, time can be used more wisely which can include engaging in more immediate and important affairs. Energy, which is wasted on problems which at present have no solution in sight, could be directed more intelligently to constructive situations.

This does not mean you should resign yourself to them, as one would in moments of despair, but you will be incapable of making reasonable judgements if you are so deeply affected by them that they menace your peace of mind. Once you are satisfied that you have done your best, you should then leave the outcome to fate. If the contemplation of a particular fear produces no positive results and continues to be a source of apprehension, you would be advised to forget it for a while and concentrate on other matters.

THE POSSIBLE, YOU DO TODAY. THE
IMPOSSIBLE, YOU DO TOMORROW.
PLATO

Individuals who are optimistic have general self-confidence and are more likely to overcome difficulties than those who are pessimistic. If pessimism is acquired by reason, there is more logical reason for optimism, than for pessimism.

THE REAL DANGER IS NOT WHAT YOU
FEAR, BUT THE EFFECTS OF THAT FEAR.

Many fears are the result of lack of planning for the future. Everyone should have a constructive purpose to improve themselves. Without it, life could become destructive. The absence of ambition could cause fears as it could destroy an essential ingredient to happiness.

Many people are anxious and ill at ease only because they have withdrawn from life. This can make them more fearful instead of having a positive outlook in all situations. Their misfortunes could be an inevitable result of past neglect.

HE WHO DOES NOT PLAN FOR HIS
FUTURE WILL FIND TROUBLES RIGHT
ON HIS DOORSTEP.

CONFUCIUS

Boredom

Boredom is a normal part of our life and is essentially an absence of pleasures or excitements, together with a comparison to more agreeable times. It is a necessary experience which we should learn to endure, yet many of us are desperate to find relief from it. We cannot expect each day to be exciting and to produce new pleasures. If you continually have a craving for excitement, then the lack of it could lead to intolerable boredom. It can be compared to drug addiction which demands a daily dose. Even though there maybe sufficient funds to engage in continuous pleasures, these can eventually become as intolerable as continuous work. If you wish to acquire a feeling of security, you will have to learn the pleasures of being by yourself. There are times when nothing is more companionable than one's own company.

Stable pleasure and fulfilment can be derived from solitude, which is generally the way of life characteristic of creative thinkers. Solitude promotes insight, increases one's mental capacity and gives the opportunity to improve oneself. These periods should be utilized for this purpose and accepted as a time for creative leisure.

Not everyone who is alone is unhappy, although for some people being alone is as insufferable as physical pain. Sometimes the inability to accept the monotony of boredom can produce an action paralysis and create a habit of putting important things off until a later time. The negative feeling caused by refusing to accept your boredom could delay your attention to matters which are not a source of immediate pleasure.

If one's mind is directed towards positive things, these periods can provide a wonderful opportunity to get neglected chores done. The time spent on these matters will not only alleviate your boredom, but will teach you a method of enduring it and will supply you with a feeling of relief when you complete some distasteful task.

Boredom could be compared to an alarm clock warning you of the danger of not having sufficient interests. Heeding the alarm can create an opportunity to reveal a new talent. Many successes have been built out of a positive attitude to boredom. The trouble with success is that it comes in many disguises. Boredom can be an incentive to change one's environment and, therefore, in many cases, it can be used as a source of encouragement to alter monotonous situations.

The positive effects of boredom are more likely to be attained when one is alone. Only in an atmosphere of quiet can one learn to develop a pattern of behaviour to improve one's life.

WHAT A MAN IS CONTRIBUTES MORE TO
HIS HAPPINESS THAN WHAT HE HAS,
WHICH COULD LEAD TO HIS BOREDOM.

SCHOPENHAUER

Outside events are only fruitful and pleasant when the participant is also in possession of himself.

THE MAN WHO TAKES PLEASURE ONLY
FROM THINGS WHICH COME FROM
OUTSIDE HAS BUILT UPON FRAGILE
FOUNDATIONS. EACH JOY THAT COMES
FROM THERE WILL RETURN THERE, BUT
THAT WHICH SPRINGS FROM WITHIN
ONESELF IS STEADFAST AND TRUE, AND
GROWS AND STAYS WITH US TO THE END.

SENECA

Persecution Complexes

We are all familiar with people who, despite their good fortune and good health, perpetually complain of the unfair treatment inflicted on them by others. They possess every ingredient for happiness, but have such a high level of anxiety that they develop a persecution complex.

We become suspicious when, on every encounter, we reluctantly listen to tales of their victimization, often as a result of the ingratitude of others. According to their own account they are continually being singled out to suffer mistreatment which they claim fully justifies their embittered outlook.

There are strong similarities with each complaint, the only variations are the personalities involved. They are, for no apparent reason, unhappy and envy happiness in others, who can even be in much less fortunate circumstances than themselves. They justify their chronic fears by imagining injustices of which they are always the victim but, in reality, have never suffered. Their life seems to involve a continual self-assertion against others.

They invariably receive sympathy for a while, until their credibility is exhausted, but eventually they find themselves practically outcasts. They continually search for new listeners as their friends, understanding that these are not genuine grievances, will have a tendency to avoid them. Because of their ever-increasing preoccupation with the hostility of others they derive no pleasure from what they have and their good fortune produces no benefits.

There is always a probability, if we are in any way active in this world, that we will encounter irritating experiences. We all receive our fair share of ill-treatment, but if a particular individual consistently encounters such treatment, we can safely assume the remedy will come only from an alteration in their own behaviour; the constant search for injustices, their fearful imagination and the belief that they are always a victim are of their own making.

Anticipating conflicts, regardless of their triviality, could be the result of disturbing elements in an individual's personality. This causes them to desperately search for faults in others, imagining slights which can be exaggerated out of all proportion. Obviously it is all affected by their unhappiness. Their self-centredness has given them a sense of insecurity, in contrast to happy people who maintain a disbelief of complaints of ill-treatment and are more likely to search for kindnesses in others.

It is advisable to avoid, if possible, friendships with habitual complainers who are constantly troubled by trivial misfortunes. In order to feed their irritation you could, in the unforeseeable future, be selected as a target and a new source for their complaints. Eventually they may be unable to resist voicing negative feelings about you, in doing so adding you to the list of their antagonists.

NOTHING ON EARTH CONSUMES A MAN
MORE QUICKLY THAN THE PASSION OF
RESENTMENT.

NIETZSCHE

The Cure

If you carefully conduct your activities, as recom-
mended in previous chapters, with the process of
Sigo Therapy, the fruits of which will result in a
feeling of serenity and power, you will then have
acquired a capacity to cope with *Fears, Boredom* and
Persecution Complexes. You will learn to emancipate
yourself from these hazards which have been
detrimental to your happiness. The discipline towards achievement must be unceasing, although the
process must not be hurried.

Our lives are full of pleasant and unpleasant
episodes and the practice of Sigo Therapy will
condition you to control each as they arise. Not only
will you be better equipped to handle the unpleasant
episodes, but you will derive an increased happiness
out of your pleasant ones. You will cease to be a
prisoner of your fears and dreads, which may have
been caused by a tendency to believe everything you

do is inadequate. The longer the period this slower tempo is practised, the greater the realization that, up to now, you have been missing the best of life. Your mind will cease to be pulled in all directions and will function with greater stability and a better philosophy of life. Of course, it has to be maintained consistently if it is to remain effective.

It will produce an inner tranquillity and serenity which will be a shield against disturbing thoughts. Your relaxed mind will defend you against imaginary persecutors and dismiss them as insignificant. Others do not have the desire to persecute you and most of your fears are the result of being too self-centred. We must realize that others spend less time thinking about us than we do ourselves; our activities are not that important. Our ego builds up an image which we prefer those around us to accept. However, their view of us may be illusory when compared to our own opinion of ourselves.

Sometimes you may not realize you are out of harmony with your friends. I have observed people whose personalities are completely transformed merely by a change of companions.

It is very important if you wish to have a life of serenity, excluding fears and boredom, to insist on associating with people who have similar tastes and opinions, as your mind will develop in stimulating and congenial surroundings. One can be dull in a particular clique and sparkle in another. If your opinions are seen to be totally negative, this could be the root cause of your boredom and could create fears of a dispute.

A change of friends may change your outlook entirely, although you must be careful that your new friends really do bring a new outlook.

With your relaxed tempo, calm stillness and new self-confidence will emerge to replace your past anxieties. Negative thoughts may still arise, but they will be of a less intense nature than before. Your new self-mastery will help you escape from them un-scathed, as you will no longer be at the mercy of every fearful thought. Your new peace of mind will direct you to become better acquainted with your-self.

PEACE IS NOT A LACK OF WAR, BUT AN
INNER VIRTUE WHICH HAS ITS SOURCE
IN THE COURAGE OF THE SOUL.

SPINOZA

The art of living consists of being receptively aware of each moment. Only by slowing your pace can you be wholly receptive. This theory is not merely a philosophical one, it is an experience which can be evidenced immediately and will assist you to avoid boredom or being fearful of what tomorrow may bring. No deep study is involved, you will simply be mastering your problems by mastering your emotions; confronting them before they are fully developed. Your new positive outlook will pinpoint troubles and solve them analytically, producing a guide to improve your behaviour and environment.

When you eliminate wasted energies on futile fears you will find the strain of your daily life greatly diminished. As each worry is dealt with, or put into proper perspective, it will be replaced by a feeling of new-found freedom.

Fear can be a slow killer and can exact a price which your body and mind must pay. To be fearful about something that in all probability will never occur, does not make sense. We must be spurred into action whenever we encounter a feeling of fear or boredom entering our lives. We must find some constructive occupation or interest to occupy ourselves, instead of being victims of inaction which will merely waste our energies.

WHAT WE ANTICIPATE SELDOM OCCURS,
WHAT WE LEAST EXPECT GENERALLY
HAPPENS.

DISRAELI

How to Cultivate the
Art of Serenity

XII

THE JOURNEY OF A THOUSAND MILES
BEGINS WITH A SINGLE STEP.

LAO-TZU

Have you absorbed what this book is attempting to convey? Are you convinced of the principles of Sigo Therapy? Do you believe its formula is practical? Will it open the door to the inner peace you have always longed for and release you from past anxieties? What can you learn from it? Are you willing to accept this simple formula as a positive technique to improve your life for the better?

Regardless of your present circumstances, I believe you can change the direction of your life to a more productive one in which you will acquire a calm, precise approach to meet each situation. It can be developed by anyone who has a sincere desire to rise above negative conditions. With its practice you will begin to enjoy greater serenity of mind. If, by changing your tempo, it produces a state of harmony and unity in your personality, then its success is manifestly proven. If it releases you from tension and anxiety in just a short period of time, it is certainly worthy of the attempt. This formula, if consciously practised, will result in the cultivation of an exquisite imperturbability which the Eastern and Greek philosophers taught and which will also greatly increase your capacity for awareness. You will find a new kind of concentration will set in as your mind becomes more aware. In fact, you will acquire an awareness at all times, which Goethe claimed was the beginning of wisdom.

It is very important to unify the mind. When your mind is pulled in all directions, it is virtually impossible to maintain concentration as you will work inefficiently. Through the practice of Sigo Therapy, the mind becomes controlled and the concentration on your goals become unified.

The great philosophers agreed that people will always act in accordance with their nature and must recognize what their true self is. It is like a spring cleaning of the mind. You view yourself as you really are, as though removing dust from a mirror, and you then see your face more clearly.

BETTER KEEP YOURSELF CLEAN AND
BRIGHT, YOU ARE THE WINDOW
THROUGH WHICH YOU MUST SEE THE
WORLD.

GEORGE BERNARD SHAW

The formula of Sigo Therapy will assist you to
discover abilities which previously had been lying
dormant, or which may have appeared on rare
occasions, alerting you to the possibilities within
you. You may also find the practice of Sigo Therapy
could be an important highway to understanding
yourself, opening a true path to eliminate your
illusions of yourself. One of the immediate benefits is
that you will feel more relaxed. As you continue its
practice, the more your personality will be improved.
Your new, relaxed composure will grow towards
achieving serenity. You will adopt a tolerant attitude
to situations which previously contributed to your
stress and the accompanying frustrations.

As the control of your emotions improves, your
new self-mastery will command the respect of those
who matter to you. You will acquire an air of
authority and wisdom which will, in turn, produce

tranquillity and even a magnetism which will make you feel the world is yours for the taking; that you can overcome any obstacle. In time, as you acquire a problem-solving mind, so your confidence will increase. You cannot agree with this practice, yet shirk the effort required for its success. You must sustain a discipline. The amount of success you will achieve will be exactly in proportion to the effort you devote to it. You will succeed through protracted effort and, with an intense desire for its results, you cannot fail.

Hopefully, this book has taught you a safe, simple and effective method of behaviour to enable you to achieve a new way of life which will lead you to man's most precious possession, serenity. No amount of material possessions will compensate for the lack of it. They may induce pleasure for a while, but continuous pleasure can be repetitious. Serenity is a reward to someone who has cultivated a sense of certainty and purpose and who has a feeling of unity with those around him. You will have the opportunity to discover that personal success is just as important as financial success. Without personal success serenity is meaningless.

Sigo Therapy will release tension, a new creativeness will develop and you will depend on your intuition to make decisions. Follow that intuition and it will eventually direct you to your aims. There is a process of growth and recuperation when you cultivate your power of intuition. It will teach you to store your energy. The process is continuous and proceeds during both restful and active periods. Everyone has access to their intuition and, if properly channelled, it can have a positive effect. As your intuitiveness gradually improves, you will acquire the confidence to wrestle successfully with any matter. No mind can escape the improvement which comes from a steady application to the subject at hand.

WITH CONTINUAL CONCENTRATION,
THE MIND ACQUIRES THE QUALITY OF
A LENS AND CAN PENETRATE DEEPLY
INTO ANY SUBJECT.

This of course will only happen if you train yourself to exclude any useless thoughts which enter your mind.

You will find the practice of this very excellent technique for improving your mind more beneficial than reading books on psychology or philosophy. The process cannot be hurried, yet the pressure towards its achievement must be sustained.

To achieve success, we must learn to extract the

best out of our present, regardless of our circumstances, and to concentrate less on the past and the future. We must hold and possess the fullness of life in our present day.

I am not advocating that you should not plan where you are going. My concern is for the person whose behaviour is such that,

WHERE HE IS GOING BECOMES MORE
IMPORTANT THAN WHERE HE IS.

The persistent demand for the assurance of a bright future could be responsible for an inability to live freely in the present. And what if the bright future arrives? Will you enjoy it to the full? Not if you have formed a habit of always planning yet further ahead. There is only one experience, the present experience; any other does not exist in fact.

THE ART OF SUCCESSFUL LIVING IS
CONSTANT AWARENESS THAT THE
PRESENT MOMENT IS SO COMPLETE
THAT IT REQUIRES NO FUTURE.

The only believable certainty is *now*.

Only the naive would claim that their future is assured; we are all subject to so many eventualities. There is no security or certainty in our lives and our determination to achieve security may be a contributory factor, or even the main reason for our insecurity.

No philosophy exists which can protect us from unforseen dangers. We cannot resist the inevitable. We have to accept insecurity as inescapable and inseparable from our lives and the answer is not to ignore that from which we cannot escape. We must be realistic and acquire a behaviour pattern to ease the impact of adverse circumstances.

I believe the technique of Sigo Therapy can supply you with the wisdom to accept an uncertain future. People of fearful dispositions are less able to meet adversity than those who retain calmness at all times. With the relaxed mental attitude which emerges from its practice, you will cultivate control and self-mastery and it will be difficult for events to unbalance you. You will be trained to cope with all situations, and will be less discouraged if adversity occurs. You will be able to absorb pain in exactly the same way you experience pleasure. Our lives consist of both, and unfortunately, these cannot be separated.

IF WE STRIVE FOR PLEASURES ONLY, TO
THE EXCLUSION OF PAIN, WE WILL BE
DISAPPOINTED.

By the careful practice of Sigo Therapy your adverse situations will become more tolerable and you will be more adept at overcoming obstacles. You must learn to bear your ills without being overcome by them.

When your mind is calm and serene it acquires stillness and seldom do everyday events disturb it. Someone who has sufficient presence of mind to bring into force instantly all knowledge will be superior to him with the same knowledge but slow recall. Even when enduring unfortunate circumstances, that calm stillness remains. It will be a protection against adversity; you can achieve it by the continual practice of Sigo Therapy.

This is my easy-to-practise formula and philosophy to help you achieve serenity. It will teach you to live objectively, develop a width of interests and secure happiness. It requires very little effort to put into practice but the gains, happiness, contentment and success are great.

The door to serenity faces you; the only effort

required is to open it. It will lead you to new contentment and inner happiness and an effortless approach to reaching your goals free from stress.

This is not a formula to be held in reserve for times of crisis, but a way of life to be practised at all times. Practice alone is the means of success and its results are in proportion to the confidence you have in the outcome.

By realigning your physical and mental energies through a complete change of technique, you will learn to conduct every action with total attention and awareness, thus opening the door to a new world of serenity.

This prospect should motivate you to set definite personal goals and to establish a plan of discipline for its fulfilment. You should resolve to heed the advice of Lao-Tzu, founder of the Taoist Philosophy, and ancient Chinese advocate of peace and quiet. He said that the journey of a thousand miles begins with a single step.

TAKE THE FIRST STEP AND PREVENT
YOUR FUTURE FROM BECOMING A
REPLICA OF YOUR PAST.

Follow this and your spirits will be elevated to that peaceful state of mind, without which, life would be meaningless and worthless;

SERENITY